Soulmate Relationships

ULLI SPRINGETT

D1502571

PIATKUS

Also by Ulli Springett

Make Your Dreams Come True
Symbol Therapy
How to Find Your Soulmate

First published in 2003 by
Judy Piatkus (Publishers) Ltd
5 Windmill Street, London W1T 2JA

The moral rights of the author have been asserted

A catalogue record for this book is available from the British Library

ISBN 0 7499 2319 9

Edited by Krystyna Mayer

Phototypeset by Action Publishing Technology, Gloucester
Printed & bound in Italy by
Legoprint SpA

Contents

Part III – Keeping a Soulmate

Acknowledgements

My deepest thanks to my Buddhist teachers Garchen Rinpoche and Rigdzin Shikpo. You taught me everything I needed to know to be happy. Many thanks to Jutta, Elke, Richard, Frank, Christine, Barbara and Juliane, who explored with me all the topics that make a romantic relationship into a happy one. Many thanks to Willi and Dorte Trienen for Buddhist and Taoist teachings. Thanks to all my clients who trusted me and were brave enough to put into practice what I suggested. A special thanks to Gabriele Schneider for ongoing good advice. And above all, thank you to my husband and soulmate Nigel.

Introduction

My own parents divorced when I was fifteen, and from then on until the age of around twenty-seven I was a relationship cynic. I found marriage laughable, and only started to change my mind when more and more people in my life committed themselves to one special person, and I found myself increasingly alone. However, I still had to work through a huge amount of inappropriate attitudes and expectations before I would become deeply happy with my soulmate and husband Nigel.

Being a practising Buddhist has certainly helped me to realise this aim, as it brought home the basic truth that love is the only way to find real happiness. It also taught me about the law of karma, which says that we always get back what we give out. In addition to my Buddhist training I attended numerous courses on the secrets of Taoist sexual techniques, which taught the amazing possibilities of using sex for spiritual development.

I did, however, find that these Eastern spiritual teachings on their own, wonderful as they are, were not enough to enable me to understand all the intricate dynamics that occur in romantic and sexual relationships between men and women in the Western world. Unfortunately, Buddhism, like all Eastern religions, does not focus on soulmates and has not much to say about romantic relationships. In Buddhist countries people often still live in arranged marriages or as monks and nuns, and the Western ideal (and ensuing problems) of a relationship that should be fulfilling on *all* levels doesn't have a place in traditional Buddhist teachings. Taoist teachings and practices on sexual energy are extremely fascinating, but they don't deal with the more emotional and psychological dynamics between men and women. I thus found that I could use Buddhist and Taoist practices for my spiritual development in general, but that I needed additional teachings to fulfil my wish to find and keep a truly fulfilling soulmate relationship.

When I trained as a counsellor, I was particularly interested in systemic and family therapy. I found that it offered the missing link needed to integrate the highly spiritual ideals of love and compassion with what happens between real men and women in the 21st century. As time went on I began to understand more clearly what is necessary in order to live in a truly happy relationship, and I found myself more and more able to predict the outcomes of the relationships of the many people I knew. Of course, my predictions weren't always appreciated, so I kept them mostly to myself. However, more often than not everything I had foreseen came true, and I used my insights to counsel people who were open to my help.

Romantic relationships can seem terribly complicated, particularly if you have a long line of unsuccessful liaisons behind you. But I found that there are four main dynamics that will almost guarantee a very happy relationship when fully understood and carefully put into practice. These dynamics are:

1. Commitment to love and to grow in love.

2. The law of an even deal.

3. Harmonious and erotic patterns between female and male energies.

4. The unavoidable merging process between two people.

Once you are able to recognise the working of these patterns in your own and other people's relationships you will find it much easier to correct attitudes that lead to suffering, and to stick to behaviour which will bring lasting happiness.

This book has three parts. In the first part I explain the working of the four essential dynamics of a soulmate relationship and compare them with the typical dynamics of ordinary relationships, which so often end in boredom or divorce.

In the second part I guide you through all the necessary steps required to find a person you can be truly happy with. I have observed that everyone who was successful in finding a soulmate has used these steps, be it consciously or unconsciously. They can therefore help you as well if you are serious about wanting a true soulmate relationship.

In the third part I explain in detail the stages every romantic relationship has to go through, as well as all the ingredients you need to stay deeply happy, inspired and passionate with your soulmate as the years go by.

In a book about soulmates I couldn't avoid writing about men, women, masculinity and femininity in general, and some of these generalisations might seem a bit bluntly carved. Some people might not find themselves in these descriptions at all. Don't be deterred by this, as these explanations are only meant to be typical examples. Obviously they are not true for everyone in all circumstances. They are also not meant to exclude gay and lesbian lovers. If you love people of your own sex, I suggest that every time you read 'man' or 'woman' you replace it with 'person with more masculine energy', or 'person with more feminine energy'.

In that way you can use everything in this book about men and women for your relationships as well.

Harmonious romantic relationships are extremely important because they are the starting point for peace the world over. Loving couples can produce loving families and loving families can produce peaceful societies. Bearing this high aim in mind, it is worth going through all the things that are necessary to overcome our personal obstacles to lasting love and happiness with our true soulmate.

Part I

Understanding Soulmate Relationships

Chapter 1

The Dynamics of a Soulmate Relationship

A true soulmate relationship is like an exquisitely beautiful flower that only grows in a well-cared-for and protected place. This flower has a wonderfully delicate scent that will enchant anyone who comes near. The joy and happiness of two people who are entwined in a true soulmate relationship can radiate far beyond the boundaries of their personal communion, and reach the hearts and minds of those who are longing for hope and truth.

The bad news is that true soulmate relationships are rare. The likelihood of finding a genuine soulmate totally by chance is just as low as coming across the exquisitely beautiful flower by accident. You can consider yourself *very* lucky when it happens.

The good news is that you can cultivate this special flower in your own garden. All you need to know is where to get the seeds, and how to plant, nourish and protect your plant. Although soulmate relationships are as precious and as wonderful as a gift from heaven, you can definitely *learn* how to establish this piece of paradise in your own life. But before we go into detail about how to find such a soulmate, let's look at what is meant by this idea a little more closely.

SOULMATES WANT AND NEED EACH OTHER

All things in the universe start at the level of mind, which means that first there has to be an idea and a wish before things can come into material existence. For a soulmate relationship it means that two people need to have a wish to be together before it can happen. This seems to be a pretty obvious insight – however, I have rarely met a person who was single and who wasn't sometimes in a dilemma about whether to wish for a partner, or to stay on their own and try to become more 'complete and independent' in themselves.

It seems to be a general human trait to be torn between striving for independence and autonomy on the one hand, and for deep and loving communion with a loved one on the other. There is good reason for this dichotomy, because both possibilities can be equally enticing.

Emotional autonomy, for example, bears the prospect of never being hurt again by another human being. For some people that sounds very good. After all, the biggest hurts most of us have experienced were inflicted on us by people we loved and wanted to be close to. I can totally understand when someone says, 'Enough is enough. From now on I will try to be independent so that this pain can never happen to me again.' Real soulmates have, however, gone beyond these fears and willingly take on the risk of being hurt again and even of being totally heartbroken. They have given up the need to protect themselves from possible emotional pain by trying to become 'autonomous', and they totally and whole-heartedly admit their wish and their need for each other. Doing this needs courage.

You might have come across the idea that two people have to be 'complete' in themselves before they can have a good relationship, or even that they must celebrate a 'mystical marriage' in themselves before they can find true happiness with a real partner. These ideas imply that you have to inte-grate your male and female side in order to overcome your neediness for the other sex and thus avoid lots of problems with a potential partner.

This all looks good in theory, but in my view it is completely beside the point. If someone really succeeds in being complete in themselves, all their need for a partner *disappears*. A person who has found everything in themselves is either a spiritually highly evolved being, or simply androgynous and without strong needs or passions. For someone like this the wish and the need to have a close and sexual relationship with another person is neither necessary nor particularly beneficial. Imagine a magnet that has 'integrated' its positive and negative poles. Such a magnet wouldn't attract or be attracted by any other magnet, and neither would a person who is 'complete' in themselves.

It is the very *in*completeness in ourselves that draws us to people who have in their characters the qualities we are missing, and creates the wish in us to unite with them lovingly on all levels – sexually, emotionally, mentally and spiritually.

The wonderful news is that there is *nothing* wrong with being incomplete or with having needs and desires. On the contrary – in a soulmate relationship we can use these very desires as the burning fire that, when united with the fire of our partner, creates so much heat that it propels us far beyond our personal limitations. A soulmate relationship is actually a means of bringing out the best in us and making us more complete and whole over time than we have ever been before.

On the other hand, two people who are in a relationship and trying to be as independent and autonomous as possible will never be able to ignite this fire. They don't use the possibility of creating a vast amount of energy through their mutual exchange on all levels. It is their holding back that creates the problems and not their desires and their needs for each other.

'That all sounds terribly dependent,' someone might

argue, 'and it was this very dependency that ruined my previous relationships!'

Let me tell you that we are all dependent in every single respect in our lives whether we like it or not. We are dependent on food, air and shelter, and we are dependent on other people in numerous ways. Any flower will always be dependent on water, soil and sunshine in order to blossom, and there is nothing wrong with that!

It is not the dependency that is the problem – dependency is simply a fact of life. It is our inability to depend on the 'right' people, on people who are equally dependent on us, so that we can create relationships of mutual support instead of one-sided dependency. What we need is *inter*-dependence – not independence. We need to learn to find a partner with whom we can team up and build mutual support, rather then being dependent on someone who doesn't want to admit their needs to us and will let us starve.

There is, however, one type of basic independence that people who want to live in a soulmate relationship do need: they must be able to leave if things get nasty (although it never gets truly nasty in genuine soulmate relationships). The basic capacity to stand on one's own feet is an important prerequisite for anyone who wants to experience higher forms of love. If we can't say 'no' and if we can't walk away when basic commitments are broken, sooner or later we will get into trouble. An ability to live alone, if the worst comes to the worst, is crucial.

Let me summarise: there is nothing wrong with feeling needy or incomplete. It is exactly these feelings that will draw us to our soulmate, so that we can be complemented by another person who is different from us and has what we want to have. In ordinary relationships people frequently hold back their needs and desires for each other, so that their union is often incomplete even on the sexual level. Soulmates, on the other hand, own their needs and desires for each other joyfully, and are able to exchange energy on

all levels: sexually, emotionally, mentally and, most importantly, spiritually. This brings out the very best in both
partners.

THE COMMITMENT TO LOVE AND TO GROW IN LOVE

How do people succeed in being deeply happy together
long-term despite all the odds, despite the ever-increasing
divorce rate and despite the fact that most people don't
know 'a single really happy couple' in their personal lives?

Some people assume this elusive happiness can only take
place in the unlikely event that two people are so similar that
they will naturally never have any conflicts or power struggles. However, this assumption can't be quite true because
we have just seen that two people are drawn to each other by
their differences rather than by their similarities. A man who
is a lot in his head will be drawn to a lively and emotional
woman rather than to someone who is as dry as he is. A
woman who feels many insecurities in herself will be drawn
to a man with a stable and strong character rather than to
someone who is as afraid as she is.

There will rarely be strong and erotic unions between
people who are similar in every respect, because those
people tend to be friends rather than passionate lovers. If
you are a woman you probably like to have girlfriends who
are so similar to you that you can enjoy (and moan about)
the same things together. But would you like to have a lover
who would be as upset as you are about his weight and his
increasing wrinkles? Probably not. In this respect, you want
someone who is masculine and *different* from you.

There is, however, one area where people in any relationship need to be similar in order to stay close. This is the area
of values, ideals and deep interests. These determine a
person's level of maturity, and we usually find that two

partners match in their level of personal and spiritual development.

Two people *feel at home* with each other when they share the same values and interests, while *the attraction* to each other is brought about by their differences in character.

As an example, people who share the same religious beliefs and interests feel at home with each other, but for emotional and erotic attraction they would need to be different in character as well. The special combination of similarities in values and differences in character makes for stable and lasting relationships, because these mutual ideals can be used to get over most conflicts. On the other hand, if two people have no ideals and interests in common even minor disagreements can lead to the break-up of the relationship.

Sadly, having mutual values and interests in life is by no means a guarantee that a relationship will be a happy one; it will just ensure that it will be stable and enduring. There are very strong (but ever so unhappy) partnerships between very immature men and women who agree on abominable values like 'men are useless' and even 'women deserve to be hit'.

Unfortunately, many people are not very clear about their deepest values and those of their partner, and it is therefore difficult for them to deal with the problems that arise from any incompatibility. But in order to find and live in a deeply happy and harmonious relationship, an awareness and conscious choice of one's deepest values, aims and interests are paramount.

Only if someone has conscious positive values can they choose a partner with similar ideals, and if this person is sufficiently different in character the relationship will be stable and happy at the same time.

What is the purpose of your life and what do you want and value more than anything? If you find this question difficult to answer, think about what you would like to maximise in your life above everything else. For example, some people like to maximise fun and sex, so they choose a partner they can have as much passion and fun with as possible. Others like to maximise financial security, and look for a partner who will share these values so that they can build wealth together. Others still want to maximise being successful, and define success as having an impressive career and three highly achieving kids.

Real soulmates want to maximise love. It is their deepest purpose to grow in love and overcome any inner obstacles that might hinder its expression.

Soulmates have as strong a dedication to love and true happiness as our beautiful flower has a dedication to the Sun. This exquisite flower will always turn towards the Sun and grow and stretch towards it. Then it will unfold petal after petal until it is fully open, exposed and vulnerable to its source of strength, and in the process it will become more and more beautiful. It is the same with soulmates: they turn to their own heart and to the heart of their partner with ever-increasing openness, rawness and vulnerability, and this delightful process profoundly beautifies and enriches all levels of their relationship: their sexual union, their affection for each other and their mental and spiritual inspiration.

It is the deep commitment of *both* partners to love and to grow in love that makes an ordinary relationship into a soulmate relationship.

What do I mean when I speak of love? Like everything else in the universe love starts initially with an idea and an intention. When we love someone we simply begin by wishing that they may experience deep happiness, love and joy themselves. When our wish is consistent and strong enough, it develops into a beautiful feeling that widens our chest, opens our heart and makes us happy like nothing else in the whole

world. Loving each other means always having these beautiful wishes for each other and for ourselves, too.

**Love in a soulmate relationship means consistently caring
for the needs of our partner *as well as* we care for our own
without ever wavering from this attitude.**

In other words, soulmates love themselves as much as they
love their partner. They don't compromise on their own
happiness for the sake of their partner, yet they always make
sure that their partner is as well cared for as possible. By
comparison, in ordinary relationships, one partner is generally more egotistical than the other, who takes on a more
self-denying role.

Soulmates understand that their partner can't *give* them
complete happiness, because they know that this can only be
found by turning inside and finding the riches that come
from their own awakening heart. They therefore usually
engage in some form of personal development or on a path
of prayer and meditation. In this way they can overcome any
inner challenges like anger or jealousy, which would otherwise spoil even the best intentions to be a loving partner.

Embarking on such a path of inner development is called
growing in love. It enables soulmates to see their relationship as a path of learning instead of expecting it to be perfect
at all times. It is this patience and willingness to grow in love
that helps two partners to get over any obstacles in their way
and find the happiness everyone hopes for who wishes to
find a romantic partner.

The love of true soulmates doesn't stop with their partner
or even with their children – it goes far beyond the small
circle of family and intimate friends. It is in the nature of
genuine love that it is not discriminating. You can be *attached*
and *loyal* to one person and reject someone else, but you can't
genuinely *love* someone and really hate another person. It's
not possible because love is like the Sun – once it is shining it
shines on everyone. Let me put it this way: soulmates are

dedicated to loving *all* beings, like our flower is dedicated to showing its beauty to everyone without any discrimination.

Would you like to experience the benefits of unlimited love for a moment? You can try this exercise.

To Experience Boundless Love

- Make yourself comfortable and relax for a few moments.

- Start by wishing to be truly happy, to experience wonderful joy and love, and for your deepest wishes to be fulfilled. Go really into this wish with feeling, and imagine that it has come true. You might experience a melting and a softening feeling around your heart, and even some tears welling up. Enjoy these feelings.

- Make the same positive wishes for all your loved ones and for your friends. See in your mind how your own happiness is enlarged so that all these people are included.

- Now, without thinking or changing your feeling, pass it on to all the people you find difficult. Wish for them all the happiness and the love of the world and understand that this will make them into better people.

- Then enlarge your positive wish and feeling to all the people who live in your town ... in your country ... in the whole world ... and finally to all the beings in the entire universe. Be careful not to strain yourself. Go back to the positive wishes for yourself in case you loose your own warm and happy feeling.

- In a last step visualise your wish and your feeling of love travelling boundlessly throughout the whole universe, which has no limitations. Stay in this state as long as you like.

How do you feel now? Would you like to live in a relationship that will help you to keep up this wonderful feeling
continuously and under all circumstances?

Everyone can develop boundless love and you don't necessarily have to live in a soulmate relationship in order to
accomplish it. However, when you can share love with a
truly well-meaning partner it will make things so much
easier.

Many people get a taste of a true soulmate relationship
when they have just fallen in love, because this is the time
when they are more dedicated to love than ever. However,
at the end of this glorious phase there usually comes a time
when one or both partners starts to regard their own needs
as more important than those of their partner. After
indulging for a few months in a whirlpool of love, old
friends, career or other things gradually become more
important again and with this often comes a decrease in
dedication to love.

In a soulmate relationship both partners will keep their
commitment to love even if their initial sexual attraction has
worn off a little. In that way they can grow in happiness,
contentment and meaning as the years go by. If this process
is successful they will even learn to look beyond personal
weaknesses and ageing skin, and will become more and
more able to see into the essence of their beloved – into their
divine nature. In this way, relationships between soulmates
can become a major accelerator in the overall personal and
spiritual development of two people, because they will learn
to see their own true nature and that of other people, too.

This process is only possible if there is a deep commitment
to love. If this is present two soulmates can advance very
quickly towards their highest unfoldment. In ordinary relationships, on the other hand, there is usually a reduction of
happiness and care for each other because of the wear and
tear of daily life. Instead of seeing more and more of each
other's beauty, the partners become more and more focused

on each other's shortcomings and react with irritation or withdrawal. As a result, their love for each other steadily decreases, which is of course very sad.

Imagine that true love is like a beautiful light that shines on top of a mountain. While most people run across the mountain in hundreds of ways without paying much attention to the light on top, those who are dedicated to love are walking only in the direction of the light. They are walking uphill towards their final destination of love and compassion, and even though the journey can be strenuous and difficult at times they are basically very happy.

Soulmates have the chance to make this journey together. If one of them falls, the other will be there to help them up. If one partner grows tired and frustrated, the other will remind them of their wonderful aim at the mountain top that is worth all the effort. On the other hand, running across the mountain and pursuing lots of different aims can look easy and amusing from the outside, but it feels much less meaningful on the inside and it doesn't bring real happiness. All spiritual seekers across all traditions have always agreed that deep happiness comes only from one source, and that is moving towards more love. True soulmates know this secret and have dedicated their lives to it.

If *you* want to live in a soulmate relationship, the first step is to choose to value the pursuit and the development of love and true happiness above anything else. In this way you will be preparing the soil that will one day be the flower-bed for the most beautiful and exquisite flower of a blossoming soulmate relationship.

SOULMATES ARE BEST FRIENDS WITH EACH OTHER

I am often astonished and also a bit saddened when I hear how little some people share with their spouses. Many people come to my counselling practice with lots of complaints about their partner, but when I suggest that they talk about their problems with their partner they often refuse vehemently. It is not only their problems that they hide from each other; they also don't talk about their personal dreams or values, or even about their most immediate worries. In a relationship like this, romance and sexual passion are impossible.

Best friends talk to each other about *everything* and so do soulmates. Honest, trusting and humorous communication is as essential for soulmates as water is for our beautiful flower. Without it, both the flower and the soulmate relationships would quickly wither.

Unfortunately, it is not always so easy to talk to each other in an honest and trusting way. Developing more love is a beautiful and romantic idea, but in practice this high aim needs a lot of dedication and even more patience. It is not enough to only love the qualities of our partner that we find beautiful and admirable; we need to be sympathetic and loving with our partner's problematic characteristics as well. If we can show each other our weaknesses without the fear of being criticised and judged, and if we even feel safe enough to joke about our problems, we are on the best way to becoming real best friends.

To be a trustworthy confidante for all the worries and grievances of a partner is one of the most important qualities that will make an ordinary partner into a true soulmate.

Equally, the readiness to share our most intimate dreams and worries can be one of the most loving gifts we can give to our partner.

To be that open with our partner is not something we can do once and for all – attempting to do this needs to be a continuous process in the same way that our flower needs continuous watering. This kind of intimate communication can be quite challenging and even scary at times, but I have never said that it is totally easy to live in a soulmate relationship. The journey to the light of love on top of the mountain goes uphill, and needs effort, commitment and often discipline as well. One of the most important disciplines is to hold back destructive criticism and anger about the shortcomings of our partners so that they can feel totally safe in our presence.

To talk in a way that takes into account our partner's needs and wishes as well as our own is an ability that you can learn, and throughout this book you will find all the necessary details to reach this aim. You can learn to be a trustworthy confidante for your partner and equally you can make sure that your partner gives you the loving support you need so that you can find the courage to share your deepest secrets. In this way you will have the wonderful fortune to have a partner who will be your best friend as well.

SOULMATES ARE TOTALLY COMMITTED TO EACH OTHER

Being vulnerable and sharing your deepest secrets; being totally dedicated to deep love and allowing yourself to be dependent, all this is risky – very risky. As most people know from bitter experience, you can be hurt more than anything if you open yourself up in love and your love is rejected or betrayed.

I don't recommend that anyone should surrender in this deep way without proper safeguards. It is just not wise to buy the most expensive and exquisite flower and then to plant it *outside* your garden fence, where it can easily be stolen or trampled on. What the garden fence is for our beautiful flower is commitment and integrity for partners in soulmate relationships. After all, as a soulmate you

voluntarily risk being totally heart-broken if things go
wrong, so it is wise to take as many precautions as you can
in order to protect the increasing vulnerability of your
opening heart.

The strongest commitment we can give and receive is a
solemn and public promise to stay loyal and loving to our
partner in good times and in bad until the end of our lives.
In our society this promise is of course the wedding vow
(and luckily more and more societies acknowledge marriage
between gay people as well).

I once met an old friend who I had not seen in years
and she told me, beaming all over her face, that she had
found a wonderful boyfriend and that they were each
others 'love of their lives'. 'Wonderful,' I said, 'do you want
to get married?' 'Oh, no,' she replied with hardly concealed
contempt, 'we don't need a paper from the state to love
each other.'

I just chuckled inside because my friend didn't know that
marriage is not about *getting* something from the state. On
the contrary, getting married is first and foremost about
giving something, giving the deepest and most whole-
hearted promise of your whole life. It is understandable that
many people are afraid of this. Those two little words 'I do'
can be the door into a prison and they can cause more hurt
than any physical injury if they are broken, but conversely
they can also open doors to immeasurable joys.

In the past famous philosophers and poets like Jean-Paul
Sartre and Kahlil Gibran have advocated the idea that true
love can only flower beautifully without the restraints of
marriage. They didn't understand that our words have
power, and that a solemn and public *promise* to love each
other has far more weight and meaning than even the most
beautiful but momentary *feeling* of love. A heartfelt promise
comes from a much deeper level of a person than any feeling
ever can, and therefore a strong commitment will give two
partners the opportunities to grow with each other in a

deeper way and to unlock more of their potential. This is true even though this promise is broken so often and by so many people. Marriage is surely not a guarantee for lasting love, as we all know, but it is nevertheless necessary to create the vessel in which we can dare to be more and more open and thus come into contact with our deepest nature and potential.

Moreover, the commitment of soulmates goes beyond the basic promise of being loyal and loving towards each other. If two people want their flower of love to fully blossom they need to be sure that their partner can be relied on long-term in everything they say. One important commitment, for example, is to agree beforehand that both partners will seek counselling if they cannot sort things out on their own. In this way they can be assured that there will be help available if they become too entangled in their conflicts.

Not long ago I read a book about sacred sex in which the author recommended surrendering during sex in ever-increasing ways 'even if your husband betrays you about important things'. I was shocked because this advice seems more like an instruction for codependency rather than for the experience of sacred sex. Did the author not realise that through such a betrayal our beautiful flower would be trampled on and probably destroyed beyond the possibility of repair? Total surrender and sacred sex can only happen when there is the deepest possible trust between two people – otherwise the commitment to love is just lip-service, rather than wonderful reality.

Let me summarise: if you want your love to grow beautifully on a long-term basis, you need strong and clear boundaries. No one should be lured into giving 'everything' in a relationship with someone who can't really be relied on and who doesn't want to give a deep and reliable promise of commitment.

SOULMATE RELATIONSHIPS ARE DYNAMIC

Fairy-tales usually end with the wonderful words 'and they happily lived ever after', and the same is certainly true for soulmates. However, unlike in fairy-tales, there is a condition for this happy ending for soulmates living in the real world. People made of flesh and blood can only be truly happy together if their commitment to love is true and strong on a *continuous* basis. Unfortunately, this commitment is not something you can make once and for all and then forget about; it is a challenge of every day and even of every minute.

Beautiful and unspoiled love comes to most of us effortlessly only in the first months of the honeymoon. Later, when demanding toddlers crawl between our feet, when our partner looks knackered and doesn't feel like sex and is anyway more preoccupied with earning the money or getting their figure back, love can sometimes seem more like a duty than a gift. If one of the partners repeatedly fails in their commitment to be loving and caring at all times, the relationship will become unstable just as any ordinary relationship will.

This is not the only danger. Whereas partners in ordinary relationships stay more or less the same, soulmates are committed to developing their full potential in order to find more love and true happiness. If one of the partners goes far ahead in this quest and the other partner doesn't catch up, the relationship becomes uneven and unstable. All couples who want to develop together spiritually encounter this problem. If they don't want to hold each other back, they have to develop more or less at the same pace. If one partner learns to be more peaceful and wise, the other has to follow suit; if one of them finds a way to overcome all sorts of personal hang-ups and develops much more inner happiness, the other has to come along as well.

To follow our partner in their development can be wonderful, but it can be ego-challenging as well. Although we all long for more love and happiness, we equally want to stay just as we are and don't want to make sometimes diffi-cult changes in order to find a new level of maturity. Let me give you an example to illustrate this dynamic.

Jim and Jane have a peaceful and caring relationship, but they also have some personal problems. Jim is often depressed and unhappy in his job, and Jane has many fears and sexual insecurities. Then one day a friend of Jane's inspires her to come along to a powerful self-development seminar and she comes back a changed person. She sparkles with energy, wants to do many new things and encourages her slightly reluctant partner Jim to come along. Even in bed she has become so daring and passionate that it is suddenly Jim who is the one who is holding back.

In an ordinary relationship Jim would now probably discourage Jane from ever going to any seminar again – her sudden change would frighten him because it would endanger the peaceful but limited stability of their relation-ship. But if Jim has a commitment to love and true happiness, if he and Jane are soulmates, he will seize the opportunity and enrol in the same or a similar seminar so that both of them can embark on a new and exciting adven-ture of finding new possibilities in their life.

Then, a few years later, Jim discovers meditation and his whole outlook on life changes. He suddenly sees the possi-bility of finding an inner happiness he never thought was possible. He develops much more equanimity, which makes Jane's emotional life look like a roller-coaster ride. Now it is Jane's turn to follow her partner in his new devel-opment, and to put her argument that 'she already knows everything she needs to know' to one side.

While ordinary relationships aim to be as static and stable as possible, soulmates develop and grow just like our flower develops one wonderful blossom after another. There is no limit to this process, and as soulmates we can embark on a journey with ever newer and more wonderful possibilities.

Soulmates Have More Than a Happy Relationship

If two people really succeed in being loyal and honest with each other, as well as being committed to the development of love and true happiness, the positive outcome will radiate far beyond the limitations of their own relationship or even beyond their family. Instead they will generate an enormous amount of energy between them that they can give to the world effortlessly, and they will inspire others in many ways.

Let me put it this way: our beautiful flower is more than plant cells, water and colour. Beyond its basic structure it will radiate beauty, grace and an enchanting scent that will inspire anyone who has the eyes to see it and the nose to smell it. In the same way a couple who has found true love is more than two people in a happy relationship. Like in a nuclear fusion, they will become able – as the years go by – to unleash a huge amount of energy and inspiration that they can use to contribute to the world. Each partner will bring out the best qualities in the other, and through their mutual support both partners can achieve many times more than they would have been able to achieve on their own.

An ordinary relationship, by comparison, can prevent people from achieving *any* happiness if the two partners have no real commitment to love. Even if one of the partners suddenly wants to develop in a positive direction the other partner will usually try to hold them back. But in a soulmate relationship both partners are able to speed up their personal and spiritual development tremendously and achieve the happiness and the love we all dream of.

Soulmates Accept the Reality of Death

If you succeed in finding a truly wonderful soulmate who is in every way the partner you could wish for, life suddenly can seem painfully short. 'We have *only* forty years together if we live to a normal age,' someone might say, and twenty years later the prospect of having *only* twenty more years together can seem even more painful.

These feelings of attachment are normal, but true soulmates can learn to go beyond them. They know that building a wall of autonomy around their heart in order to protect it is no solution. Instead, they learn the high art of holding in themselves a deep love for their partner while clearly knowing that they must loose them one day. The outcome is an extraordinary feeling that is deeply fulfilling and exquisitely painful at the same time.

Soulmates know what it feels like to loose someone because they are confronted with the inevitable loss of their beloved partner every day of their lives. They are not ignoring this fact, and neither are they trying to protect themselves from it. It is this union of love and pain that is the source of all compassion. If two people in love learn to use their fear in the right way, it will make them full of empathy for the pain of other people. Therefore soulmates are not only deeply happy together, but also full of compassion for anyone who is suffering.

Moreover, if two people in a soulmate couple are open to the idea of life after death, they don't need to despair over their inevitable loss of each other. Instead, they can see each other's passing away as only temporary, and can make strong wishes to meet again in their future lives. These wishes will have a great influence on how they will live in their future, and will give even more meaning to their present life together.

Chapter 2

The Law of an Even Deal

The universe works according to very simple laws, the most important of which is the law of 'an even deal'. In Buddhism this law is called 'karma' and basically it means that you get back what you give out, that every cause you set in motion will bring about its appropriate effect. Our Western equivalent says, 'What goes around comes around', or 'As you sow so shall you reap'. For example, if you shout at your friends each time you feel frustrated, you will soon be very lonely. Equally, if you work hard the odds are you will have a good career.

Sometimes the working of the law of an even deal can be intricate and difficult to understand, because cause and effect can be years apart from each other and you will have no idea why you are suddenly hit with a personal catastrophy or with surprising luck. But at other times you will get an immediate result, as is the case, for example, when someone has a fling and promptly gets a divorce.

The Buddhist teaching about cause and effect holds the key to being successful in any area of your life as well as in romantic relationships. In the following sections I explain how it can be applied to everything that is happening between two partners.

THERE IS ALWAYS AN EVEN DEAL BETWEEN PARTNERS

If we could take everything two partners give and say to each other and carefully weigh it up, we would basically find that this exchange amounts to roughly an even deal. For example, both partners might show the same amount of affection to each other, or one partner may earn the money while the other stays at home and looks after the children. We would also find that as long as this deal remained roughly even the relationship would most likely continue. It is as if each one of us has a little calculator in our head that measures exactly (consciously or unconsciously) all giving and taking with our partner, and makes sure that at the bottom-line we get out of a relationship roughly as much as we put into it.

This doesn't sound very romantic, but I'm afraid it's what we all do. There have been many psychological studies which show how we all tend to choose partners who are equally attractive as we are, equally educated and with similar backgrounds. In partnerships where these areas don't match, we usually find other, more hidden deals of giving and taking that make up for the areas of unevenness.

Some people may not agree with me on this idea, and will claim that they gave many more times than their partner did and only peanuts came back. However, if we want to analyse the dynamic of a seemingly uneven relationship we need to look at it a little more closely.

If a match between two partners doesn't seem equal at first sight then we have a more hidden even deal. If someone really didn't get anything out of a relationship they would simply leave it. The very fact that they don't is a sign that no matter how unfair and difficult the relationship seems from the outside, it is better for the participants to stay together than to split up. The even deal in such a relationship could be something like: 'I am so afraid to be on my own that I will do much more for you than you do for me as long as you don't leave me,' or 'I believe in the Bible and it says that women need to submit to their husband. Although this seems unfair I am doing it because in that way I will get a better after-life.'

Another example of a hidden even deal is the well-known scenario of a beautiful young woman who marries an older man, but only if he has enough money and status to match her youthful looks. A young man can also be attracted to an older woman because of her emotional maturity and sexual experience, but he will rarely marry her if there are no other benefits for him. This all sounds terribly unloving, I know, but I am not inventing it. I am just describing reality.

'But what about abusive relationships?' someone might ask. 'They can hardly have an even deal.' No matter how destructive a relationship looks from the outside, on the inside you will always find an even deal. The abused partner (usually the woman) often has such low self-esteem and is so afraid of living alone that she will bear 'anything' to avoid a break-up of the relationship. The even deal she shares with her partner says, 'I am such a worthless person that I'll agree to put up with anything, as long as you don't leave me.' Such an attitude is of course very sad, but the relationship will continue as long as both partners continue to share this attitude and their deal remains even.

The even deal applies to every area of a relationship, but first and foremost it is built around the most important values and interests of both partners. Someone who values money more than anything would never marry a poor person, and someone whose highest value is personal freedom would never go near a person who desperately wants to get married, even if they are the most attractive individual in the world. If a man believes a woman will only stay with him if he fulfils all her material desires he will attract a woman with a similar attitude, and together they will have a relationship that looks quite unfair from the outside, but for them on the inside is an even deal.

If you look at relationships from this viewpoint you will come to understand that couples tend to match each other as keys match their keyholes. Even if they argue; even if one of the partners complains that they have been taken advantage of, deep down they always match in two main areas. This ensures that they both feel that at the bottom-line they are both getting something out of their relationship. The two main areas in which partners match are:

- They consciously or unconsciously share some important values and interests, which indicates their level of maturity.

- They match in the even deal they have built around these values.

Let me illustrate this with an example.

Liz and Jim share very similar values in life and they both want more than anything to be rich, to have status, and to have a big, impressive house and two highly educated children. Liz has Christian values and regularly goes to church, but these values are less important to her and don't interfere with the materialistic attitude of her husband.

This set of ideals provides Liz and Jim with a strong foundation for their marriage, and helps them to get over the many emotional disagreements they have. In order to earn the kind of money they want, Jim works sixty to seventy hours a week in an extremely stressful corporate environment, while Liz runs the household and brings up the kids. They both feel they are getting an even deal with their role division, and they exchange money and status with emotional and practical support.

Liz and Jim also share some less conscious values about housewives not being equal to their husbands. Liz, for example, doesn't have access to her husband's accounts and has to ask him whenever she wants to spend a bigger amount of money, while Jim goes out and freely buys the latest electronic gadgets he desires. Liz complains about this unfairness to her girlfriends, but deep down inside she doesn't feel she has the right to ask for equality and puts up with the situation while grumbling silently.

Despite having a stable marriage, two highly achieving kids, a grand country estate and holidays at the most expensive beaches in the world, Liz and Jim not surprisingly feel quite dissatisfied. They both feel emotionally unfulfilled and frustrated that they can't be happy, despite the fact that they have more in life than most people they know.

As you can see, Liz and Jim's problem is their set of values, which provides them with material success but can't give them the happiness they really want. The trouble is that many people have little idea which values would lead to real happiness, so they are constantly running after a host of goals that will leave them dissatisfied in the long run. Soulmates, on the other hand, know their aims and values in life, and have understood that only love can bring them deep fulfilment. If they are wise they create a working even deal in their relationship that will guarantee it is both happy and stable.

WHY RELATIONSHIPS GO WRONG

Most trouble or dissatisfaction in romantic partnerships can be traced back to one or two reasons:

1. The relationships are difficult or break up because the law of the even deal is violated.

2. The relationships are difficult or break up because the commitment to love is not strong and reliable enough (which means the partners don't *really* wish each other well).

Let's look at number one first. The even deal extends to every part of the relationship: giving each other emotional and practical support, showing affection, sharing the finances and the household chores, and all other areas. For both partners to be happy there needs to be an overall equal giving and taking in the relationship, but it doesn't need to always be in the same way and at the same time. Maybe one partner supports the other more financially and the other does more of the childcare. Or one partner listens more to the other and gets a lot of appreciation in return. Sometimes both partners take it in turns to develop their careers while the other has a more supportive role.

The complexity of this situation makes it likely that the law of an even deal can be violated in many different ways, thus leading to problems and even to the break-up of a relationship. The following list can give you an idea why and how these types of problem arise and how they can be avoided. In Part III I explain in more detail how the diffi-culties which arise from violating the even deal can be resolved.

How the Law of an Even Deal Can Be Violated

One partner continuously gives less than the other

It is obvious that giving your partner less than they give you will cause them to grow frustrated over time. Always giving less can have two reasons: firstly it can be the result of pure selfishness. It should be clear that this attitude is unsuitable for achieving happiness in any area of life.

Giving less can alternatively be due to the fact that a partner is *not able* to give more for whatever reason. If you want your relationship to be happy, you can remedy this unevenness by being very appreciate of your partner when they do more for you than you can do for them. Then the law of an even deal is put into practice and there shouldn't be any reason for you not to have a happy relationship. But if your partner doesn't get your appreciation it will probably become very frustrating for them and your partnership will be at risk.

One partner continuously gives more than the other

It is less obvious why giving more than your partner on a long-term basis may cause your relationship to eventually break up. Some people might assume that it would be nice to be at the receiving end in a partnership, where they can just take, take, take. However, all this taking is only nice in theory. In practice, it often works as a mounting burden of debt for the receiving partner. There is a clear limit to how much we can receive from someone before we start feeling uncomfortable. We might feel an increasing sense of duty and guilt about not giving anything back, or we might get annoyed because all the receiving disempowers us and places us in the role of a helpless child.

Can you see how this dynamic can take place even if both partners love each other? A woman, for example, can feel a great sense of love for her partner, but by doing too much for him (for example giving him money and managing too many of his affairs) she can cause him to be unappreciative and even angry at her because he feels patronised and disempowered. And if the woman doesn't understand this dynamic, she herself will feel undervalued and like a victim. Doing too much for your partner is the core issue in code-pendent relationships.

One partner is too submissive and self-sacrificing

In all the relationship break-ups where I have seen the man leave the woman, in ninety per cent of cases the woman had been very submissive. Why would that be? Why would a man leave a submissive, self-sacrificing girlfriend or wife with whom he can have it his way all the time? The reason is that men like submissive women only in theory or maybe in their sexual fantasies. In real life they get bored pretty quickly with someone who doesn't have their own mind and just does everything he says and wants. And women get turned off by a submissive man even more quickly.

If you are submissive you are holding back your opinions and your whole life-energy, and you therefore limit drastically the amount of giving and taking in your relationship. Even worse, the suppressed energy has to go somewhere and usually it comes out in indirect aggression, for example in small but vicious acts of sabotage, or in an illness that can be ruthlessly exploited to impose guilt feelings on the more dominant partner.

Unfortunately, it has again become quite fashionable to suggest that submission by the female partner will put an end to the rising divorce rate. In reality, being too submissive is one of the main reasons for relationship break-ups.

One partner is dominant and their partner's needs are not met

Are you one of those people who know what they want and are not too shy to ask for it? I am like this and I had to learn through bitter experience that you just cannot expect your partner to be the same. As we have discussed before, people are drawn to each other by their differences and so quite usually a more dominant and headstrong person finds themselves in a relationship with a more easy-going partner. The latter is much more often undecided about what to do, and easily gives in when confronted with the strong desires of their more dominant counterpart.

Although this looks like a convenient arrangement from the outside, over a longer period of time it will almost certainly backfire. Suddenly the formerly laid-back partner starts to complain about having had to go for long country hikes for years, although they've never enjoyed them. Or a female partner may complain that he has always touched her sexually in a certain way although she really hated it. If the imbalance is even stronger, the more compliant partner may withdraw or even leave the relationship.

The only way to prevent this from happening is for the more dominant partner to *continuously* make sure that their partner's needs are met. If you are a person with a strong will you need to ask your partner forever: 'Are you happy with this? Are you really sure you don't want something else? Please say what you want.' This will seem a bit contrived at first, but it is the only way that a more dominant character can make sure that the law of an even deal will not be violated.

One or both partners is unforgiving

You have to be very careful to apply the law of an even deal in a beneficial way if your partner does something wrong or hurts you. First of all, it is not conducive to use the law as in 'an eye for an eye and a tooth for a tooth' because this would quickly lead to a downwards spiral where both partners became increasingly mean and unloving to each other. If we can never forgive our partner when they have over-reacted in the heat of an argument, and try to punish them with anger or many days of ice-cold silence, we will have won nothing, although we would seemingly be obeying the law of an even deal.

Where one partner hurts the other, therefore, the law of an even deal is best adhered to when the 'guilty' partner apologises, brings presents and makes any amends as best they can. After that the two people can be even again and the past should not be regurgitated in every new argument. By apologising and making amends and then forgiving, the law of an even deal is adhered to in a way that leads to happiness rather than to more sorrow.

One partner is too forgiving

It is hard to believe this, but there is actually a danger for a relationship if one partner is *too* forgiving. Many people who are on a spiritual path of some kind assume that it is 'wrong' to get angry with other people and that inner peace comes only from forgiving. In principle they are right – if it weren't for the law of an even deal. If your husband, for example, does something hurtful like calling you names in a heated argument or neglecting his share of the childcare, you won't really do him a favour if you 'just' forgive him. This is because he won't be able to make amends and get rid of the guilt he will feel unconsciously or consciously.

If one partner is often hurtful or unfair and the other never gets angry and never demands amends, the relationship will become more and more distant. The seemingly 'forgiving' party will secretly grow more and more resentful, while the guilty party will want to leave the relationship and find a new partner with whom they will have a 'clean slate'.

In order to obey the law of an even deal, both partners must always insist on amends before they forgive something negative. In that light, getting angry with a partner can sometimes actually help them to redeem their guilt. Only if both partners are even again will they be able to remain close after unfortunate things have happened.

One partner receives less but doesn't ask for equality

Women often complain to me that their partner is not very loving and giving, but at the same time they are unwilling to ask for more. Instead, they do what women have done throughout the centuries: they sulk, they silently resent and most often they simply withdraw their affection, doing so in the hope that their partner will sense the imbalance and start giving something back. However, throughout the centuries we have witnessed that this strategy usually doesn't work. You can read in the next chapter on male and female energy why this is so.

Basically, the partner who receives less, be it man or woman, has the responsibility to make sure that the law of an even deal is adhered to by asking their partner for more and insisting on equality. If this is done in a gentle way and without criticising your partner, it can often work wonders.

One partner demands more and more

Unfortunately, the limits of every relationship are dictated by the partner who wants to give *less*. No matter how much you demand, no matter how much you give in the hope that something will come back, and no matter how loving and patient you are – if your partner does not want to give more there is *nothing* you can do.

This is the lesson everyone needs to learn who has a tendency to codependent relationships in which people go on suffering with totally unsuitable partners. Applying the law of an even deal in such a case means carefully looking at what your partner wants to give to you voluntarily. If this is not enough, you need to *ask* them *gently* to give more. If the answer is 'no', you have to decide whether you can live with this without building up subtle grudges, or if you would rather look for a new and more giving partner.

Asking for more can only lead to happiness with a partner who *wants* to give more, and if the asking partner is willing to give as much as they want to take. Where this happens, both partners can actually experience a large increase of giving and taking which can make them both very happy.

One partner is too autonomous

There is nothing wrong with being very independent as such – but in a partnership it can lead to severe imbalances. The person who is very autonomous doesn't need as much support and affection as their partner, and because of this they prevent their partner from giving to them. Again, having an autonomous partner who doesn't need a lot might sound good in theory, but in reality it deprives you of the very best of a loving relationship, which is to make your partner happy. If your partner is already happy without you, there is nothing left for you to do and you might as well leave. Women or men who repeatedly give their partner the message 'I don't really need you,' mustn't be surprised when their partner suddenly finds someone else with whom they can finally make a real difference.

This obviously doesn't mean that happy and independent people are disqualified from having a fulfilling relationship. But they should take great care to constantly reinforce their appreciation of their partner, and to value whatever their partner is able to give them. In this way they will be obeying the law of an even deal and their relationship will flourish.

Both partners give less and less to each other

As much as giving more and more leads to a wonderful upwards spiral in every relationship, giving less and less leads to more and more dissatisfaction. Unfortunately, it is the latter dynamic that happens in most ordinary partnerships, and this is a key element in the growing dissatisfaction that many couples experience as the years go by. If, however, both partners give less and less they are still obeying the law of an even deal, and therefore the relationship (although dissatisfying) can still be quite stable.

This dilemma cannot be resolved by one partner suddenly starting to give much more, because this would make the relationship rather unstable for the reasons I have already given. It would be much more beneficial to sit down together and talk openly about how the romance and the support of each other has decreased, and then to make a *mutual* decision to *both* start giving more to each other. This can seem a little bit contrived at the beginning, but it is the only way to stop the slow death of a partnership that will occur if two people give less and less to each other.

Both partners give back exactly what they have received

A relationship where both partners give back *exactly* what they have received is stable but not very dynamic and probably pretty boring as well.

The law of an even deal leads to most satisfaction if both partners give *a little bit* more to each other every now and then.

In order to have a thriving soulmate relationship both partners need to be interested in inner growth towards more love and happiness. In this way they will be able to inspire and surprise their partner in many new ways. With every bit of inner happiness that you discover for yourself you will have more to give to your partner, and with every step of your partner's inner growth they will help you to see the sparkle of joy in everyday life.

How the Commitment to Love Each Other can be Violated

A while ago I discussed the law of an even deal with an acquaintance and she found the whole concept a bit fishy. 'I don't understand all this talk of an even deal,' she said. 'Shouldn't we try to be more selfless instead?'

The answer is no. Trying to be selfless is a contradiction in itself because 'the self' cannot try to be 'self*less*'. This strategy will only result in self-*denial*. It has led millions of people (mostly women) into codependent relationships with uncaring partners because they didn't dare to insist on having their own needs met. 'Trying' to be selfless makes people feel resentful and victimised – consciously or unconsciously. It is much more healthy for both partners to be determined to carefully implement the law of an even deal.

'But what about love?' my acquaintance insisted. 'I don't think it is desirable to say to someone that I will only love them as much as they love me.'

My acquaintance is right; the love and the positive wishes you feel for your partner are not a part of the even deal. Love that is bound to conditions and is given only when your partner behaves in the way you want them to behave is not love. It's manipulation. The even deal in a relationship only

applies to everything you and your partner do or say *openly*
to each other.

**The love in your heart and the amount of good wishes you
have for your partner are not part of the even deal.**

In other words, you can create problems in a relationship by
doing too much for your partner, but you can never do
anything wrong by *loving* them too much. You can even love
a partner once you have split up. The more love you feel in
your heart the better it is for you as well as for everyone else.

The real problem with love, however, is that people love
each other too little. Once the honeymoon period wanes
people can start, little by little, to regard their own well-
being as being more important than their partner's and all
too easily, smaller or bigger traces of selfishness can slink
into the relationship. If this happens their commitment to
love is violated and the happiness in the relationship starts
to go downhill.

Sooner or later this lack of love will also show openly in
harsh or cold words and egotistical behaviour, and the law of
an even deal will be violated as well. Under these circumstances it is impossible to create a soulmate relationship, and
if the egotism of one or both partners goes far enough the
relationship might even break up.

Let me summarise: loving each other means wishing your
partner well and regarding their well-being to be as important as your own. The more love you feel for yourself and for
your partner the better. The law of an even deal applies only
to everything two partners say or do to each other *openly*,
and it says that two people can only find happiness in their
relationship if their overall give and take is even.

Investigate Your Past or Present Relationships

Once you have a basic understanding of the law of an even
deal and the commitment to love, and how their violation
can destroy any happiness between partners, you can start to

apply these concepts to your own past and present relationships. If you look at them from this point of view you won't need to pay a relationship counsellor to tell you why your relationships may have failed; you will be able to come to your own conclusions.

To Investigate Your Relationships

- Call to mind one of your romantic relationships that you found difficult or dissatisfying and find out what went wrong by asking yourself two questions:

  1. Was there a true commitment to love each other?
  2. In what way was the law of an even deal violated? Remember, the law is always violated by both partners, so check how you and your partner fitted together 'like a key in a keyhole'. For example, if your partner gave much less than you did, then you gave them far too much.

- Go through all your difficult relationships and analyse why they went wrong. Don't judge yourself for these problems and break-ups, but rejoice that you now have an efficient tool at hand to avoid such difficulties in future.

- Now look at all your romantic relationships that were (or still are) very satisfying, and analyse why this is so. You will certainly find a commitment to love and a satisfactory balance in the overall giving and taking in these relationships.

The law of an even deal is such common sense that I sometimes wonder whether to mention it at all. However, you only have to go into any toddler group once to hear many women complaining about how much more they are doing in comparison with their husbands, and how unfair it is that they have to ask to spend money while their husbands can go out and buy anything they like. And when you go to a working mothers' group the complaints are even worse.

I have talked to several full-time working mothers who earned far more than their husbands, organised the entire childcare and did most of the housework themselves. However, whenever I dug a bit deeper it turned out that these women had been pivotal in implementing this unfairness and they couldn't be bothered to sit down with their husbands and find a better role division. Although they were carrying a whole lot of unremedied frustration, deep down they believed that they had no other choice and that the deal they had with their husbands was in some strange and contorted ways 'even' enough.

THE EVEN DEAL IN SOULMATE RELATIONSHIPS

Interestingly, many people who are on a spiritual path of some kind don't like the idea of an even deal in relationships very much. Instead, they favour the idea of boundless and selfless giving, and aspire to let go of any expectations that something should come back. No one, however, can afford to ignore this law because it is at the basis of the dynamic that makes every aspect of the universe tick – and in particular relationships.

I have seen 'ever so spiritual women' who tried to relate to their partners in 'ever so selfless ways', but struggled with low self-esteem and made continuous 'pricking' remarks at their partner's expense. Similarly, I have seen 'ever so spiritual men' who continuously threatened to leave their wives and their children in order to pursue their ideal of boundless love and compassion on their own in a meditation cave in the Himalayas.

These 'spiritual' men and women were unable to integrate their high ideals of boundless love with the reality of having a relationship and family in the real world. The 'spiritual' women couldn't accept that they had needs themselves that usually surfaced in very unpleasant ways if they were suppressed for the sake of their sacred ideals. The 'spiritual' men didn't understand that their progress to enlightenment would only be as substantial as their ability to keep a loving commitment to others. They needed to realise that a broken promise would hinder their development many times more than an honest trial to integrate their spiritual ideals with the reality of screaming toddlers and the hectic world of family life.

If we want to live in a soulmate relationship in which we can develop spiritually and emotionally *with* a partner we need to focus on developing as much love as we can *and* to understand the law of an even deal and apply it skilfully in our relationship. In other words, even the most idealistic spiritual people need to learn that they can only receive if they are willing to give, and that they need to be kind to themselves in order to be kind to others.

Applying the commitment to love and the law of an even deal in a soulmate relationship means saying, 'I love you so much that I will never put my own happiness before yours, and I love myself as well so that I will never neglect to unfold my potential or allow myself to be taken advantage of.' This means *always* finding those compromises that make *both* partners happy.

Soulmates know that their relationship will work best if they both give each other *a little bit more* every now and then, because this will slowly increase the overall giving and receiving.

It is not a good idea to 'try' too hard to be totally selfless and forgiving, or to inundate your partner with help, advice and financial support, because this would put the receiving partner under pressure. It is much better to increase the overall giving and taking in a relationship slowly and carefully by sometimes giving a *little bit* more than you partner, and by forgiving only after your partner has sincerely apologised.

In order to achieve these goals, soulmates usually talk a lot about their feelings, and if they have to apply the guidelines about love and the even deal they are able to quickly resolve any arising disharmony.

Chapter 3

Male and Female Energy

I was brought up in the Sixties and like many girls at that time I was told that I could do anything that men do if I only wanted to. Parents and teachers alike rejoiced in the new freedom to teach their daughters and female pupils that they were as good as any boy, and that there was no fundamental difference between the sexes.

As liberating as these concepts were at the time, they were painting only part of the picture and they have created many new problems for both women *and* men. The truth is that although men and women both have female and male energy, there are still strong differences between the sexes. What we hadn't been taught was to develop deep confidence in our feminine side and to express it freely. And although men have been taught to respect women in male roles, they often have not been shown how to value the feminine side of a strong woman while also enjoying their own masculinity.

In order to experience truly satisfying relationships we need to be confident in our own gender identity and to have positive feelings about the other sex as well. It is just not possible to experience romantic and erotic passion without the expression of feminine energy as a woman and masculine energy as a man. These two opposites need each other in order to ignite romance and sexual feelings as much as wood needs oxygen to ignite a fire. These dynamics apply equally for gay and lesbian couples – here as well, one partner usually identifies more with feminine energy and the other more with masculine energy.

The best way to think of femininity and masculinity is to see them as talents or as natural inclinations. Most women have a talent for being feminine and most men have a talent for being masculine. However, every person also possesses the opposite energy and can learn to develop it. The trouble starts if we are not allowed to express our natural inclinations because the current fashion says that women have to be super-strong and that men who freely enjoy their masculinity are like brutes.

Feminine energy

Feminine energy is like the sky. It is open and can embrace many things and people. There is a stillness in feminine energy that is not passivity but receptivity and responsiveness – and an attentive 'being there'. The core of femininity is surrender – a voluntary process of letting go that is highly pleasurable. Surrender has nothing to do with submission, which is suppression in a self-denying way. Surrender is really the opposite of submission because it means to become more and more oneself in the most satisfying way. Deep surrender is the art of enjoying things intensely. Therefore a very feminine woman can experience many times more sexual pleasure than almost any man. Moreover, the ability to let go makes feminine women more talented on the spiritual path, because surrender is more important than anything else if you want to come closer to your Higher Consciousness.

Masculine energy

Masculine energy is best described by the image of a rocket. The rocket is very active and it flies through the sky with a great sense of determination. Masculine energy is aim-oriented. The rocket doesn't just fly for pleasure but has a purpose that it wants to accomplish at all costs. Masculine men are therefore single-minded; they can put their full energy behind their goals, which they are able to see through without being distracted a great deal. Such men are also dominant and don't like to be told what to do.

Masculine men find it easier then feminine women to accomplish things in the real world because they are more goal-oriented and less distracted.

DEVELOPING MORE CONFIDENCE IN YOUR GENDER IDENTITY

Generally speaking, men and women are happiest if they can express their natural inclinations to be dominant or to surrender in all areas of their lives. I have, however, met many men and women who find it very risky, if not impossible, to live their femininity as well as their masculinity.

I once met a tall, strong and capable man who almost wailed at me that women 'didn't allow him' to express his masculinity. Equally, I have met many otherwise confident women who told me that surrendering just wasn't an option for them because it would make them feel too vulnerable. These attitudes are unfortunate, because they deprive both sexes of the deep satisfaction that comes from truly being themselves. A man doesn't need to wait for permission before he can start acting strong, and a woman who doesn't dare to let go deprives herself of one of the most pleasurable things in the world.

Some women are also locked into misunderstood feminist ideas – they assume that surrendering means loosing your personal power. Nothing could be further from the truth! A woman is completely in control over when, to what and to whom she wants to surrender. If she surrenders to her inner depth she can get in touch with her slumbering creativity. If she surrenders to her Higher Consciousness she can develop divine love and intuition, and if she surrenders to the man of her dreams she will find the deepest romantic fulfilment.

Obviously, a confident feminine woman can live her masculine side and enjoy every bit of women's liberation alongside the intense happiness that comes from the pleasure of feminine surrendering. Some men, on the other hand, think that dominant masculine behaviour is somehow wrong – as if it would make them immediately into potential rapists or killers. However, expressing your masculine, determined side is not only highly enjoyable, but it is also what most women find very attractive in a man. I have spoken to quite a few men who felt a lot of pain and outrage because they simply couldn't understand why they were constantly rejected; they themselves thought that they were just as 'nice' as women wanted them. These men didn't know that most women don't fancy members of the male sex who are 'just nice', but devoid of anything that would make them into 'real' men.

The next exercise is designed to help women and men to gain more confidence in their gender identities. It is part of the symbol-therapy method that has brought reliable and often amazing results for all sort of problems. It is a safe tool and free of any reported side-effects.

To Develop More Confidence in Your Gender Identity

For women

1. Say to yourself: 'I love myself deeply with all my problems and weaknesses, and in particular I love myself even if I am not fully confident in my surrendering feminine side.'

2. Visualise a beautiful pink lotus (seen from above) in your heart in the middle of your chest. When you breathe out,

see and feel how the colour pink radiates throughout your body and into the area around your body and finally to all the men in the world. Feel how the colour pink coming from the lotus flower in your heart dissolves all fears of being a wonderful feminine and surrendering woman. Breathe out the colour with all your love and best wishes. When you breathe in, just rest in the enjoyable sensation that comes from feeling and seeing the pink lotus in your heart. Then breathe out again and radiate the colour of the lotus throughout your being and beyond in the most loving way. Do this for two minutes twice a day for a few weeks or until you feel more confident. Be open to help and advice from whatever source.

For men

1. Say to yourself: 'I love myself deeply with all my problems and weaknesses, and in particular I love myself even if I am not fully confident in my dominant masculine side.'

2. Visualise a shiny silvery rocket (seen from the side) in your heart in the middle of your chest. When you breathe out, see and feel how the silvery colour of the rocket radiates throughout your body and into the whole area around your body and finally to all the women in the world; see how it dissolves all fears of being a strong, confident and dominant man. Breathe out the colour with all your love and best wishes. When you breathe in, just rest in the enjoyable feeling that comes from feeling and seeing the shiny silvery rocket in your heart. Then breathe out again and radiate the colour of the rocket throughout your being and beyond in the most loving way. Do this for two minutes twice a day for a few weeks or until you feel more confident. Be open to help and advice from whatever source.

Please don't change the healing symbols in this exercise in any way – they were given to me for you by my Higher Consciousness. If you are interested in looking further into Symbol Therapy and how you can receive your own healing symbols, please refer to my book *Symbol Therapy*.

If you are a woman and want to nurture your feminine side and your ability to surrender, you can do things that are physically very pleasurable, relaxing and non-goal oriented, such as going to the sauna or for a beautiful country walk. It is best to go with a friend with whom you can share your thoughts and feelings freely, until your whole being widens and opens up and you become as relaxed and all-embracing as the sky.

If you are a man and want to support your girlfriend in developing confidence in her femininity, tell her every day how beautiful she is and how much her femininity inspires you. Use every opportunity to carry a box or open a door for her. These little gestures can often work wonders. The feminine identity of a woman is centred around who she 'is' (as opposed to what she 'does'), which includes the way she looks and feels. So, never – even once (!) – criticise her emotions or parts of her body, because this would be traumatic to her feminine self-esteem. Instead, take great care to be a sympathetic listener and really try to understand how she feels.

A man who wants to become more confident in his masculine side needs to choose activities that are goal-oriented, competitive, and demand strength and discipline. This may sound a bit strenuous, but it is the only way to become like that strong and determined rocket which will definitely hit its aim and be much more attractive to the opposite sex.

If you are a woman and want to support your man in developing confidence in his masculinity, then first of all never make an issue out of it. Instead, tell him every day how much you admire his work and how grateful you are for his support. Let him carry every parcel and open every jam-jar for you, and thank him graciously. The masculine identity is centred around doing and his competence. Therefore if a man is criticised for his work it can be traumatic for his masculine self-esteem. So avoid giving unsolicited advice about how he could do things better, and take extra care to downsize any of his failures and mistakes.

YOUR GENDER IDENTITY NEEDS TO BE BALANCED

Both feminine and masculine energies blossom most beautifully if they are balanced to a smaller degree by their complementary energies.

If men are *too* masculine they can become ruthless and overbearing, and may start breaking moral and legal rules in order to achieve their aims. Such men can also be extremely selfish and totally unable to make any commitment to others. Men's singlemindedness and egotism, and the dominance of too much masculinity in them, must be balanced with the feminine quality of taking into account the needs and wishes of others and making real commitments to take care of them.

If women are *too* feminine they find it very difficult to get up and do anything in order to change things for the better. Instead, they put up with whatever comes their way while their friends wring their hands in despair at so much passivity. The biggest weakness of undiluted femininity is extreme dependency on others. Women who are *too* feminine need to develop some masculine energy, so that they can say with confidence, 'Enough is enough and I am out of here!'

If you are a woman who finds it impossible to be on your own for any length of time, you are too far into your feminine side. You will seem very attractive to a man who is too far into his masculine side and who will, by definition, be very strong, but also selfish and over-bearing. This unfortunate dynamic happens because extreme opposites attract each other. However, a selfish man is obviously the last thing you want. If you are extremely feminine you want a protective man who will take care of you. But such a man would be more mature and would have integrated some female energy. Because of this, he would only be attracted to a more mature woman who had integrated some masculine energy and would be better able to stand on her own feet than you are at the moment. This is how the law of an even deal works in relationships: you can only have a partner who has the same level of maturity as you have, because you can only get what you give.

If you are a man who finds it terribly difficult to make commitments, and the thought of marriage drives cold sweats of panic up your spine, you are too far into your masculine side. You will therefore be attracted to very feminine women who are, by definition, very surrendering, but also very dependent. As an extremely masculine man, however, you will want a woman who is able to give you some freedom and who doesn't cling to you for dear life. But a more independent and mature woman would have already integrated some masculine energy, and would only be attracted to a more mature man who can make stronger commitments to her than you are able to at the moment.

A partnership between two immature people may match perfectly but will always be an unhappy one. The typical scenario is a weak and dependent woman with low self-esteem, who clings to an unreliable and selfish man at all costs. In order to avoid this painful dynamic, but to still find the romance and erotic passion that is only possible between men and women who are confident in their gender identity, we need to integrate *some* of the energy of the opposite sex. The typical scenario then would be a feminine but confident woman who has a satisfying relationship with a strong and caring man.

A confident, feminine woman who has integrated some masculine energy might say: 'I deeply long for and need a protective and caring man, but I am strong enough to make no bad compromises and to stay on my own until I find a partner who really suits my needs and loves me.'

A confident, masculine man who has integrated some feminine energy might say: 'I love to explore and conquer the world, but I am also ready to make a deep commitment to my woman and be totally protective and caring with her.'

Some men and women who are too far into their masculine or feminine side need therapy to become more balanced, but I think most people are able to find the opposite sex in themselves just by making a strong commitment to developing it. Repeat one of the above sentences and feel in your heart of hearts whether you want to be like that. If you do, make a strong wish that you will be able to develop your missing strength, or the ability to take care of a woman, and reaffirm your commitment to your aim every day.

BEING TOO ANDROGYNOUS CAN BE AN OBSTACLE

Some people who have been single for a long time have, out of sheer necessity, developed a great deal of the opposite gender side in themselves. In particular, if you are a lone parent and need to be mother *and* father to your children, you will almost certainly develop a strong masculine side if you are a woman, and a strong feminine side if you are a man. This is a totally appropriate development under the circumstances, and it will help you a great deal in coming to terms with your demanding situation.

Bear in mind, however, that the more androgynous

someone's behaviour, the less attractive they are to the opposite sex. This happens because they are not like one pole of a pair of opposites that is searching for its other half – they are too integrated.

A woman, for example, who gives out the message that she doesn't really need a man and can do everything for herself will not attract a strong and caring man who wants to make a difference in a woman's life. On the contrary, such a strong woman will be much more likely to attract a weak man who longs to be taken care of himself. It is this process of role reversal between masculine and feminine energy that is the reason why so many strong women end up with weak men, which is often dissatisfying emotionally as well as sexually for both of them.

On the other hand, a man who easily shows his tender, vulnerable side, and who is very emotional and talkative, is often not very erotically attractive to a feminine woman. She probably likes him as a friend, but in order to be erotically attracted she needs someone who is more different from her. Another problem is that men who are very androgynous often have close platonic friendships with women. If they are reluctant to give these up once they have started a romantic relationship with someone, this can lead to jealousy.

Don't get me wrong – I'm not saying men mustn't have any female friends and women mustn't be too independent. Being androgynous is very beneficial when you are single, in a working environment, or if you are a lone parent. It can, however, lead to problems if you want to find and maintain a relationship that fulfils your romantic and passionate longings.

Most romantic relationships thrive best when the woman puts aside most of her male side and lets the man take care of her, and when the man puts aside most of his sensitive female side and is the strong caretaker that the woman desires. This is not a prescription. It simply describes what

most women and men are happiest with. It doesn't mean
that women should give up work or never speak up to their
spouse. On the contrary – through learning to be confident
in her feminine side, a woman can be equal to her male
partner *and* deeply relish a relationship that is the fulfilment
of all her romantic desires.

Deep down inside, most women have never given up the
romantic idea of finding a handsome and strong knight who
will take care of them, and men who are ready for commitment deeply long for a beautiful princess they can protect
and love. It is only when we have failed in these aspirations
too often that we become cynical and bitter, and try to
develop the opposite sex in ourselves in order to avoid
future hurt. We then assume that our romantic dreams were
foolish or wrong, or even outright sexist, and try to stamp
them out inside ourselves. It is this very process of trying to
become androgynous, however, that will prevent our
deepest dreams from coming true.

Most men will probably agree that if a woman constantly
keeps competing with them in all kinds of manly activities, if
she consistently lets them know how she could have done
everything better than they could, and if she belittles their
attempts at gallantry, this acts as a complete killjoy to
romance. Equally, there is nothing more off-putting for a
woman than a man who consistently looks to her to take the
lead, who takes a lot of time to express and explore his
tender and hurt feelings, and who is more interested in his
own looks than in hers.

Generally speaking, in order to have a deeply satisfying
and romantic relationship, a woman needs to confine her
male-dominant behaviour to situations and places where it is
more appropriate and beneficial – like her work-place, for
example. Conversely, a man needs to confine his passive and
surrendering urges to areas where they are more appropriate – meditation, for example. Let me summarise:

> **Most romantic relationships will work best if the man is the man most of the time, but is also able to express *some* tenderness, and if the woman is the woman most of the time, but can express *some* strength as well.**

'Wait a minute,' someone might say, 'I know some very successful relationships between dominant women and somewhat "feminine" men. How do they fit into this scenario?' The answer is that we have to know a lot about a couple before we can truly judge whether their relationship is romantically fulfilling for both of them.

Through my training and work as a counsellor, I have had the opportunity to talk to dozens of couples about intimate details of their relationships. It is from these conversations that I have learnt what I described above. However, let me stress again: these are just descriptions and are not intended to tell anyone how they should live their life.

MEN, WOMEN AND THE LAW OF AN EVEN DEAL

When we investigate how men and women apply the law of an even deal in their relationship we can find astonishing but fundamentally different tendencies:

- When women receive something from their husband or boyfriend, they automatically assume that it is now their turn to give something back and will feel motivated to do so.

- When men receive something from their wives or girl-friends, they automatically assume that they must have earned this favour by their past kindness; therefore they do not necessarily feel motivated to give something back in return.

- If women want something from their partner, they will often do something *for him* in the hope that he will then feel the inner urge to give something back. However, this will usually not happen because a man assumes that he deserves what he gets.

- If men need something from their partner, they will not necessarily ask for it but will withdraw and try to find a way of 'not needing it'. In extreme cases they may even start an affair with another woman who 'more voluntarily' gives them what they want.

Have you ever wondered why so many women do the entire housework as well as holding down full-time jobs, even though this is clearly grossly unfair? The answer is that a woman has a much stronger impulse to give, not necessarily because she is a saintly being, but because it is her habitual way to interpret the law of an even deal to her own disadvantage. If a woman receives something she often immediately wants to give something back in return, and if she wants something she will first do something to motivate her spouse to give her that thing, thus 'earning' her right to receive.

A man, on the other hand, will not necessarily be motivated to give because he has received a lot from his partner. If he has received too much he might feel patronised and disempowered, or even 'smothered with love', but these feelings will not necessarily motivate him to give something back. On the contrary, he is much more likely to withdraw from a partner who does too much for him because he will intuitively feel that something is not right.

This is how many relationships develop the typical conflict where 'she' is bitter because she 'does everything', and 'he' is angry and confused because he doesn't understand why he can 'never do anything right'. If this conflict is not resolved, 'she' will do even more while 'he' will grow even more distant and do even less. What is the way out of this vicious circle? Obviously, men need to learn to give more and women need to learn to do less and receive more. But how can they achieve this?

The first and most important step is to become more confident in your gender identity. A confident, masculine man will have a great motivation to give, simply because it will make him feel like the knight who takes care of his precious princess, which he will like. A confident, feminine woman, on the other hand, will be able to receive all this with grace and hold back her desire to pay everything back immediately. This will make her feel even more romanced and blissful – just like a real princess. She will also know how to ensure that her man remains motivated to keep giving by nurturing his confidence in every way. She will appreciate his actions and even admire him. A confident, feminine woman will not feel disgraced by giving her partner this admiration. On the contrary, her gratitude will be genuine and will add to both partners' romantic fulfilment – and as the man receives the appreciation of his woman he will be motivated to do even more for her.

It is the woman's responsibility to make sure that the law of an even deal is fulfilled to her satisfaction, because of her habitual tendency to interpret this law to her own disadvantage.

Both the man and the woman will feel most romantic fulfilment in their relationship if the man gives a little bit more than the woman, and if the woman keeps giving back a lot of appreciation and gratitude.

If you are a man and you groan at this idea, let me ask you two things. What gives you more romantic fulfilment: to give the woman of your dreams a beautiful red rose, or to be given a red rose by her? What makes you feel better in your manhood: to earn so much money that you can tell your partner that she doesn't need to work, or to have a wife who earns so much money that she can take care of you? Most men will agree that as nice as it is to receive a red rose or to be taken care of financially, in terms of feeling good as a man they will want to do the opposite.

Unfortunately, every now and then even the most confident and kind-hearted man will fall into the male habit of forgetting to do his share of the household chores – let alone to give his partner romantic presents on a regular basis. A confident, feminine woman knows how to deal with this.

She certainly will not be submissive and just put up with it, because she knows that if she did this her suppressed resentment would only surface at a time and place where it would be detrimental to the relationship. She knows that starting to work harder for him, or even to bring him lots of presents herself in order to motivate him to come back to the even deal, is the last thing she should do. In her wisdom she knows that this is an approach that may work on her girlfriends, but not necessarily on her man. Nor will she start to criticise her partner for failing her, because she knows that by damaging his confidence through her criticism she would be cutting off her nose to spite her face. So, what will she do?

If a man doesn't fulfil his share of the even deal to a woman's satisfaction, she must remind him in a *friendly, non-critical and non-demanding* way.

In that way the beneficial circle of him doing something for her and her being very appreciative of him can be set into motion once again. If, however, the man is very stubborn and doesn't respond to these skilful moves, the woman needs to sit down with him and explain to him in a friendly way that she wants the workload in their relationship to be distributed in a fair way. She also needs to make it clear (without putting any pressure on him) that she can only surrender to him in a feminine way if he is affectionate. Most men will accept the law of an even deal once they have understood the idea because it is a very logical concept, and they will start to act accordingly. But women have to do their part as well, and resist the temptation to either criticise their man or do too much for him.

In order to obey the law of an even deal, women and men in romantic relationships don't always need to give and take the same things. If a man gives practical support and the woman provides him with a heartfelt thank you, the law is beautifully adhered to. If a woman tells her partner a lot about her feelings, he doesn't necessarily need to do exactly the same. If he listens empathetically to her and she thanks him for doing so, the law will be fulfilled.

I know a woman who has fallen in love several times with men who have many problems, as well as severe financial difficulties. She sees herself as a very kind-hearted being, so she always lends these men money, pays the rent for them and tries to find jobs for them – all in the hope of receiving some love back.

To her great dismay things never work out. Instead of loving her, one man after another grows increasingly angry at her, and they always end up being verbally abusive. This is usually when she finishes the relationship, feeling totally hurt and confused by their 'ungratefulness'. Her last partner even stole money from her and betrayed her with another woman, and now she is totally heart-broken.

By now, you probably understand that this woman's problem is that she is constantly ignoring the law of an even deal in general, and the law of an even deal between men and women in particular. Had she been a man who gave money to a woman she might had got away with it. But giving so much to a man increasingly disempowers him, and deprives him of any form of romantic fulfilment in the relationship. The verbal abuse is just a 'natural' outcome when this unhealthy dynamic occurs unconsciously between two people.

All this obviously doesn't mean that women should never do anything for their men. But most women in our society do too much for their partners, because they have not learnt to be confident in their feminine side and don't know how to receive with guilt-free joy. Once both men and women know how to feel really good in their gender identity, their romantic relationships will be *much* more satisfying.

MASCULINE AND FEMININE ENERGY IN SOULMATE RELATIONSHIPS

In almost every society, masculine energy is more valued than feminine energy. If you are in your masculine side you are active, aim-oriented and productive, and every boss or teacher will agree that it is exactly these faculties that they want in their employees and pupils. On the other hand, the feminine qualities of being surrendering, receptive and intuitive might be viewed as lazy, chaotic and unproductive.

I think it's fair to say that men and women alike need a certain degree of maturity before they can fully understand and value feminine energy. Patience, letting go and intuition are all feminine qualities, and most people don't really value them when they are young. Many men as well as many women only develop these abilities later in life, when all their masculine fighting and struggling has not brought them the happiness they have looked for. However, as explained before, women are naturally more talented and inclined to develop and express their feminine abilities, and if they receive the right support and encouragement they can use them to find a profound and deeply satisfying happiness that also contains crystal-clear wisdom.

In Tibetan Buddhism there are repeated references to the fact that women are more talented on the spiritual path precisely because of their ability to let themselves go and surrender to something that is bigger than them. Because soulmate relationships are dedicated to these higher forms of love and bliss, both the man and the woman in such a relationship will value feminine energy much more profoundly than people do in ordinary relationships. When love and deep happiness are the highest aims of two people, the feminine talent of surrender and intuition becomes of the utmost importance.

In a soulmate relationship you can often see that the man looks with love to his woman for spiritual inspiration, and that he will use his masculine strength and power to protect and nurture her process of deep spiritual and emotional surrender. Both partners will appreciate the feminine qualities in both of them in an ever-deepening way, without devaluing the masculine qualities at all. On the contrary, the masculine qualities of both partners will enable the couple to bring the love, wisdom and happiness that they have found for themselves into the world in order to help other people.

Let me summarise: in a soulmate relationship, the masculine–feminine polarity will exist between partners who are confident in their gender identity, and this will guarantee romantic and passionate attraction between them. At the same time, both partners will value the feminine qualities of surrender and intuition much more highly than is generally the case in our society, without devaluing masculine energy in the process. In this way, soulmate relationships are a heaven for women and a paradise for men, because both are valued and desired in the most beautiful way.

Chapter 4

The Unavoidable Merging Process

If we were clairvoyant we would not see other people as solid and material bodies but as fields of dynamic and multi-coloured energy. If we entered a room full of many people, we could observe how people move and exchange 'balls of energy' between each other's energy fields even when they don't talk. We could see that some people give away energy from their own energy-fields, while others take in this energy and make it part of their own fields. We would also find that the loudest and most dominant people give out more balls of energy than others, and that the more receptive people will be taking in this energy.

If we could see even further we would realise that the balls of energy are emotions, feelings and thought concepts that are exchanged between different people. The more sensitive and receptive people are, the more they can 'pick up' these feelings from others, and sometimes this can be a nuisance – for example, they might suddenly feel gloomy simply because they are standing next to someone who is depressed. Luckily, it is not very difficult to let go of what you have picked up from strangers, and you usually don't need more than a clear determination to get rid of such unwanted feelings. There is no need to try to shut down completely in order to protect yourself, because being receptive can be a lot of fun. It can also be very beneficial, for example if you are a counsellor or a salesperson.

If, however, you are in a close friendship with someone, letting go of the attitudes or feelings you have picked up from your friend can be more difficult. If you like someone you will have fewer defences against them, and will be more open and receptive towards them than you would be towards strangers. Generally speaking, this is not a problem, because we usually enjoy receiving energy from our friends. But if a friend criticises you it will literally 'get to you', and you might have to sit down with them to talk things through.

Only if they 'take back' what they have said will you be able to feel good again. If, however, you are unable to talk to them, their critical energy ball will 'sit' in your energy field and you might try to get rid of it by having angry inner dialogues with your friend in your mind. These are normal experiences that everyone has at times, but as we become more clear and loving negative energy exchanges with others become less and less of a problem.

Now we come to the case of two people who are in a romantic and committed relationship, and are having sex with each other on a regular basis. With our clairvoyant view we could see that the energy exchange has become dramatic! And it should be like this, because we literally want the energy of another person when we feel drawn to them sexually and romantically. This is not just a metaphor. People who are in love clearly take feelings, attitudes and even bodily sensations from each other. In actual fact, the energy fields of two people in a sexual and loving relationship will merge more and more into one energy field that envelopes both people and allows both of them to draw on a much greater variety of feelings, ideas and responses to the world.

People who are in long-term loving relationships can exchange so much energy with each other that they become literally more and more alike. The woman, for example, can become genuinely stronger and more dominant without losing her soft and tender femininity, and the man can become genuinely softer and more caring without losing his masculine strength. You can even find that older and happy couples start to look more and more alike. This process, however, will never go so far that one partner will take over the complete personality of their spouse – both partners will enrich their own personalities in a very positive and healthy way.

What does all this mean when it comes to your search for a soulmate? First of all, you will hopefully become more choosy if you look at a potential partner and ask yourself not only: 'Do I like and fancy her?' but also, 'Do I want to *become more like her* over the course of the next ten to twenty years?'

Most people don't realise how impossible it is to fence themselves off from a partner. They might think that they are two separate beings, not understanding that this is definitely not true. Even if two people argue a lot, and even if their love for each other is not very strong, they will still experience a strong exchange of energy. In particular, through having sex we pass on energy to each other in a massive way; along with sexual fluids we transfer to each other feelings, attitudes and even parts of our character.

It is virtually impossible to shake off this kind of exchange like the gloomy feeling we may pick up from a stranger, because we literally merge and mix our energy fields with our partner. And, as we all know, it takes a lot of pain, effort and time to separate again. Knowing about this unavoidable merging process between partners should make us very careful about who we choose to be with in a sexual relationship.

On the other hand, the energy exchange between a couple can be a true blessing when you find someone who positively complements your missing qualities. An insecure woman, for example, can become much more confident through being in a relationship with a strong man, and a man who lacks joy and enthusiasm can become much happier if he finds a woman who enjoys life. This process is automatic and effortless, and can save you a lot of work, money and time compared with going to dozens of expensive self-development workshops.

On the minus side, two people can limit and inhibit each other more than most people are aware. Because two people in an intimate relationship are sharing a mutual energy field, one person will always be affected by what the other feels – they are sitting in one emotional boat, so to speak, and there is no real escape.

If one person is depressed or angry a lot of the time, this will inhibit the other person to a great extent and prevent them from being really happy. This is not because the unhappy partner has a bad motivation and doesn't want their partner to be happy; it is merely the outcome of sitting in one emotional boat. The longer two partners are together, the more difficult it is to just feel 'your own' feelings and 'be totally yourself'.

As a rule of thumb, you can only be as happy as your partner is.

There are exceptions to this rule, when two people success-fully disentangle their energy fields, but this doesn't happen very often. If you look at the couples you know well, you will rarely find that one is genuinely happy and loving, while the other is sitting in a bog of neurosis, depression or addiction. Partners in a couple usually match each other not only in their level of personal and spiritual maturity, but also in their level of overall happiness, and they do so even more the longer they are together.

Unfortunately, it is the more negative partner who is dominant and will determine the overall emotional atmosphere of the relationship.

Negative emotions like anger, depression and fear are

grosser and heavier than positive emotions like joy, love and happiness. Anyone who has been to a workshop or meditation retreat where they have become much more joyful and happy, knows the painful and disappointing feeling of entering the 'real (more negative) world', and seeing most of their wonderful energy slowly but surely disappear. Or maybe you have seen how one single negative person can spoil the whole atmosphere of an otherwise lovely work team.

The same dynamic happens in every close relationship. The partner with the lighter and happier emotions will slowly but surely adapt to the more negative partner. The next question is obviously: how can we use this knowledge to create blissfully happy soulmate relationships?

SOULMATES AND THE UNAVOIDABLE MERGING PROCESS

Soulmates want to maximise love and true happiness beyond everything else in their lives, and they know that they can only achieve their aim as much as *both* of them advance in their spiritual development together. They fully understand that they have only one emotional boat, and that they can only swim or sink together.

Soulmates will therefore take great care of the well-being of their partner out of love, but also out of enlightened self-interest. If you know that you can only be as happy as your partner is, their well-being will automatically become much more important to you. In every way you behave, with every decision you want to make, you partner's happiness will matter to you as much as your own, because you know that you will achieve nothing if only you yourself get your way.

Whatever you achieve, if your partner is not really happy with it, *you* will not be really happy with it either. On the other hand, in a soulmate relationship you can rest assured that your partner will behave in the same loving way to you, so that your mutual emotional boat can be a place of happiness rather than misery.

Soulmates also understand that they can easily hold each other back if they don't follow each other in their spiritual development. It is not possible for one partner to unfold their potential for love, spiritual insight and happiness, while the other continues to be miserable, mean and selfish.

Spiritual teachers and self-help books sometimes give us the impression that we can advance on the path of enlightenment no matter what the circumstances. Unfortunately, this is only half true, because a partner who resists your development can be an impediment that is almost impossible to overcome. You can spend a thousand hours meditating on forgiveness and love, but if you have a partner who draws you into an argument as soon as you leave your meditation cushion, it will be hard to harvest the results of your efforts. Even if your partner's attitude is generally less negative, you can only advance on the path of wisdom and compassion as much as they are willing to come with you.

If, for example, one partner finds a way to open up their heart and feel true forgiveness and compassion, the other partner will (or should) follow suit. As you can imagine, this is not always easy, because we often cling to our negativity, anger and selfishness with a self-righteousness that is totally inappropriate in the bigger scheme of things.

In actual fact, we are rarely more convinced 'that we are right' than when we are ranting and raging about the miserable state of the world in general and our personal surroundings in particular.

If we feel like this it is difficult to be open to the suggestion of our more serene partner to, for example, go for counselling, take up meditation or drink less alcohol. When we are feeling miserable we want to at least 'be right' about it. The last thing we want is for someone to point out that we have created this negativity ourselves and that it is our own responsibility to get out of it.

It can also be difficult to follow our partner in their development simply because we are complacent and would
rather, say, watch the telly than join our wife in her meditation. But if our commitment to maximising love and true
happiness is to be more than a lip-service, we should seize
the opportunity and join our partner in her attempt to
develop more peace of mind, inner joy and crystal-clear
wisdom.

**The best way of making sure that you and your partner
develop at the same speed is to make a pact.**

In this pact you and your partner promise to always help
each other in your quest for love and true happiness *and to
also allow your partner to help you.*

The last part of the pact is crucial, because for most people
it is a much bigger challenge to promise to accept help than
to promise to give help. Men in particular can experience
this as an admission of failure, and they can easily interpret
their partner's attempt to help as an attempt to control
them. Women therefore need to take extra care to offer their
help in a non-demanding and non-controlling way. If
their partner sticks to his agreement of maximising love,
they will have the great pleasure of having a partner who
'works on himself' and makes an effort to open up to his
whole potential.

My husband Nigel and I made such a pact part of our
wedding ceremony, and I can tell you that it is a wonderful
thing. If there was a road to enlightenment, I would feel that
we are now travelling on a free motorway (unfortunately not
always at full speed!) compared with the bumpy small roads
full of barriers and detours we were travelling on before with
other partners. To have a companion with whom you can
truly share and support each other's process of unfolding is
the most beautiful gift one can imagine.

The minds of many women are broader than the minds of
many men, and it is therefore often the female who brings

new ideas into a partnership, and who wants to try things out. A committed male soulmate will welcome these developments and will try anything out with her, from aromatherapy to crystals.

On the other hand, the minds of many men are more focused and determined than those of women, and if they find something that works they are often more able than many women to follow it through. A committed female soulmate will therefore be grateful for the steadfastness of her mate, and will hang on to his determination in order to be more determined herself.

If we are aware just how much we depend on our partner in our journey to more love and fulfilment, there is a danger of easily becoming critical. If, for example, the man is depressed for longer than the woman assumes is justifiable, she might feel a strong urge to tell him 'to buck up'. And if the woman is upset too often because of minor incidents, her partner might experience a strong tendency to ignore her. These approaches, however tempting they may appear to be, are totally counter-productive.

Women usually want to talk when they are upset. If a man wants to help his partner, he needs to learn to be a sympathetic listener, even if he would never be upset about similar things. When men are stressed out they often want to withdraw and get better in their own way. Women have to learn to give them this space, and to withhold their impulse to indulge them in too much motherly caring.

Let me summarise: in an ordinary relationship, the more miserable, stressed and depressed partner will dominate the happier one and determine the overall atmosphere in the partnership. In a soulmate relationship we find the opposite dynamic, because both partners have agreed to follow the advice of the happier partner without ever criticising each other. Soulmates therefore develop many times faster on their path to deep happiness than do people in ordinary relationships.

Part II

Finding a Soulmate

Chapter 5

Preparing the Ground

Finding your wonderful soulmate is very similar to the process of sowing a seed and nurturing it into a beautiful blossoming plant. If you have ever sown seeds, you will know that the first and most important step is to clear and prepare the soil, so that your tiny seedling has the best environment to prosper in. You can't just throw your seeds into your muddy and cold midwinter garden. You need to take a tray and put fine and clean seedling compost of the highest quality into it, and you need to clear a light and warm place on your window-sill. Getting the soil ready is the messiest and most laborious part of the whole process. But once your tray is sitting on your window-sill, nurturing the seedling is easy.

The process of finding a soulmate starts in a very similar way: the first bit of clearing and preparing the ground is the most difficult and strenuous. However, once you have created in yourself the conditions for a soulmate relationship to take root and grow, it is quite easy. You just need 'to water your wish' on a regular basis and avoid growing impatient. So, let's get to work!

Generally speaking, most people who whole-heartedly

commit to their wish to find a soulmate do so within a
reasonable time-span. However, quite a few people remain
single despite an intense wish for a partner, and sometimes
despite a lot of strenuous search activities as well. According
to my observations, these people tend to have one thing in
common: they have unresolved issues of resentment either
with one of their previous partners, or with their opposite
sex parent.

I myself have been such a case. I was betrayed in the most
outrageous way by my previous boyfriend, and it felt more
than right for me to give him the feeling that he was a really
'bad guy' by not talking to him any more, and by throwing
his birthday cards into the bin unread. I felt incredibly hurt,
and 'punishing' him like this gave me at least a minimal
feeling of compensation.

We say 'revenge is sweet', but the saying doesn't tell us
that revenge also costs us dearly. In my case, and in that of
every single person in a similar situation, it cost us a new
partnership. I was single for nearly five years, but once I let
my previous boyfriend know that I didn't hold any grudges
against him any more, it was just another six months before
I was finally 'allowed' to fall in love with my future husband.
The interesting thing is that my husband-to-be and I had
known and fancied each other for years, but some mysteri-
ous and invisible barriers had prevented us from getting
together.

The worst of all these barriers is holding grudges against
former partners or parents. Until such grudges are
removed, I feel there is little chance for someone to achieve
any deeper form of happiness, let alone to create a soulmate
relationship. In order to find a true soulmate, we need a
whole-hearted commitment to maximise love beyond
anything else, and holding grudges is just not compatible
with this aim. The following exercise is designed to help
anyone to let go of these major barriers.

To Let Go Of Old Grudges

- Make a list of your former partners and add the name of your opposite sex-parent.

- See in your mind these people one by one entering your room, and notice whether you feel any anger, fear and depression. (Fear and depression are anger that has turned against yourself.)

- Say to every person you feel negative towards, in turn, '[name], although I still don't condone your behaviour, I will now stop holding grudges against you so that we can both be free.' Visualise a sharp knife cutting through the ties of your negative feelings that are still binding you to this person.

- Write or speak to everyone you felt resentment towards, and tell them that you don't have any negative feelings towards them anymore and that you wish them all the best.

Sometimes this exercise can be difficult, in particular if you haven't spoken to your former partner in years. But letting go of these negative feelings and telling your ex-partner about it is like opening a door – the *only* door through which your soulmate can come to you. It is the door to your heart, and if your heart is still closed because of your old bitterness about your past relationships, there is simply no way in which you will be able to fall deeply in love again.

HOW TO FINISH YOUR PREVIOUS RELATIONSHIPS

The next step you need to take in order to prepare the ground for your soulmate relationship is to finish all your previous relationships in the best way possible.

People hang on to their previous partners in numerous ways, for example through guilt, regret or resentment, and all these lingering involvements are obstacles to a new relationship. We have already dealt with resentments, but if you feel strong guilt or regrets about what has happened between you and your former partner, you also need to get in contact again and offer at least a heartfelt apology. If possible, do whatever you can to make good whatever you have done wrong in the past. People usually underestimate how much they are holding *themselves* back when they have a bad conscience about something. Having no luck with finding a new partner is only one symptom of this unfortunate dynamic.

In whatever way you are still attached to a former partner – through blame, guilt or grief – you need to resolve and let go of these negative attitudes before you can move on to the more positive part of finishing a past relationship.

The best way to finish a past relationship is to find something to appreciate about it. Only then will you become free for a true soulmate.

To Finish Your Past Relationships in the Best Way Possible

- Take your list of your previous partners and opposite-sex parent.

- List all the positive things you have received from each person, for which you are grateful. Maybe you learnt something from an ex-partner, or perhaps they supported you in some way. Think only about the good times, and include things you would normally take for granted. Your parent, for example, gave you life, which is the greatest gift of all.

- Wish your former partners and parent well for their future.

People who have done this exercise have come up with the following:

'Although my marriage didn't work out we now have two wonderful children who I love very much.'
'My ex-wife supported my career.'
'My ex-boyfriend introduced me to a person who is now an important friend of mine.'

From now on, whenever you think of one of your past partners and negative thoughts and feelings start to overwhelm you, go back again and again to the positive things about the relationship you are grateful for. And don't blame yourself for staying too long in a former relationship – you just did the best you could, given the circumstances and your state of maturity.

Thinking about the positive things in a former relationship can also be helpful if you feel strong longings for a former partner and 'just want them back'. If you can really appreciate the things you got from this person, it is easier to accept their decision to go their own way.

Focusing on the positive and wishing your ex-partners well for the future requires a certain discipline. If necessary, read through the above list as often as you need to in order to regain basically good feelings about them. Remember, only positive feelings will set you free to do whatever you want. The ties that bind you are your own negative feelings of grudging, guilt, bitterness, self-blame and lingering attachment. I am not the only person who could only find her heart's desire once I had plucked up my courage to phone my old boyfriend to say in a few friendly words that all negativity from my side had stopped. I've seen many other people going through this wonderful process, and moving on in leaps and bounds once they had left their old burden of negative feelings behind.

MOVING OUT OF FAMILY TRAPS

If you study family trees, you will find it quite incredible to learn how certain patterns in behaviour are passed on from generation to generation. There are families who have at least one alcoholic or one suicide in every generation. There are families in which at least one sibling out of every generation stays unmarried, and there are families in which there are lots of famous and highly achieving members over many generations. Moreover, every family in itself creates more or less rigid role assignments for each of its members, which can be difficult to overcome. There is usually one victim in the family, one hero (your maddening sister who has achieved everything), a rescuer, often a clown and many other roles as well.

Another unfortunate dynamic is 'suffering on behalf of other family members who had a hard destiny or an early death'. Very sensitive children often take on the pain of others because of a misguided sense of love. It is as if they say, 'If my mother had a terrible sex-life, I will not have one either in order to be loyal to her.' Or, 'Because I took the place of my older brother who died early, I will not live a fulfilled life in order to be loyal to him.' Achieving more wealth and happiness than other members of their family can cause some people to experience enormous guilt feelings, and unfortunately many people choose to stay in the limiting but secure boundaries of what is 'normal' in their clan.

These roles, dynamics and 'inherited' family patterns can best be compared to spells that have an incredible power as long as people believe in them. It can be creepy to study how deeply destructive types of behaviour are passed on from one generation to the next, and are repeated in an automatic and unconscious way. Fortunately, it is not that difficult to move out of these patterns and to break these spells. The only thing you have to do is to recognise the 'family curse', and to make a conscious decision to lead a better life. It really is as simple as that.

If you suspect that the fact that you have not found a partner is to do with being caught in a family trap, it is worth doing some research into the dynamics in your family. Interview as many relatives as possible and look out for people, dead or alive, who had similar destinies to yours. Is it possible that you are repeating an old family pattern? Or are you denying yourself a fulfilled life because you have taken on the suffering of someone else who was ill, died early or was excluded from the family because of their 'bad' behaviour? Have you always been the 'problem case' or the 'rescuer' in your family, which allowed your siblings to take on more favourable roles?

If any of this rings a bell with you, all you have to do is to make a conscious decision to break this negative spell and live a happier life. Family traps can only have power over you as long as you allow this to happen. So make a new decision and – even more importantly – stick to this decision, no matter what. Your life might not change overnight, and I promise you that your family members will try to make you go back to your old role. But if you refuse gently and persistently and stick to your new decision for a happier life, there is nothing they can do.

One word of caution: moving out of family traps can only be done successfully if you manage to not close your heart to anyone and become resentful again. If your family research leads you to become even more bitter and depressed, nothing much will be achieved. But every problem, every rejection and every hardship that is endured with an open heart will make you into a stronger, wiser and happier

person than you would be if you had not suffered at all. In
that way, no suffering will ever be in vain. It holds an inher-
ent and beautiful reward for you if you manage to be
empathetic, understanding and clear at the same time.

THE DANGER OF BETTER-THAN-NOTHING RELATIONSHIPS

There is only one more step you need to carry out before
your seed-tray sits nicely on your window-sill. You have to
make some space for it and clear away all the things that are
in its way. In terms of finding a soulmate, these blocks are so-
called better-than-nothing relationships. These are, as the
name implies, relationships with someone who you don't
love fully and who doesn't really love you, but with whom
you feel better off than you would if you were on your own
and had 'nothing'.

Despite the fact that relationships like this can be convenient, they are not better than nothing. In actual fact, they are
worse than nothing. If you are with someone who doesn't
really love you and who doesn't whole-heartedly feel that
you are their most desired partner, you live with a constant
self-confidence destroyer. And you do the same for them.

Remember the unavoidable merging process between two
partners? In a better-than-nothing relationship, a couple are
constantly giving each other the message that they are not
really attractive or loveable. It is only a matter of time before
both partners internalise this message and thus become literally less attractive and less loveable. This outcome is
definitely worse than living alone and using the time to find
your inner riches through contact with good friends, and
through exploring and loving yourself.

In order to avoid worse-than-nothing relationships, many
people need to make a strong commitment to stay true to
their deep wish of finding a real soulmate with whom they

can be happy on *all* levels. This high aim can only be achieved if they avoid anyone who would be second best for them.

Letting go of better-than-nothing relationships and being on your own can be frightening, and we will deal with this problem in more detail later on. But don't get me wrong, I am not recommending that you live as a monk or a nun until you find your dream partner. On the contrary, allowing yourself to have some fun can be very beneficial and enhance your confidence and joy of life, as well as your attractiveness.

But making commitments to one person while secretly looking for someone better is a barrier to finding your soul-mate. For one thing it is not fair on your partner, and for another it will be very bad for your self-esteem because you will be allowing someone to treat you with less love than you wish for. If you get involved with someone who is not your soulmate, be honest about it. If this person agrees, you can be friends who share the amount of intimacy that feels right for both of you.

Chapter 6

Sowing the Seeds

Have you ever noticed that people live in totally different worlds? For one person the world is a dismal place full of loneliness and rejection, while for another the very same world is a place of love and fulfilment. For yet another, it might once have been an empty desert that is slowly changing into the most enchanting oasis.

What is causing people to perceive our world in such different ways is their own deep beliefs about it, the way they act on these beliefs and the feedback they get from their actions. In other words, the way we perceive the universe can be likened to a garden that we have sown with the seeds of our own thoughts and deeds. The same is true for our relationships.

Our present and past relationships are a direct outcome of what we believed about men, women, relationships and ourselves.

For example, if you believe that most women are just after your money, you have probably already met many very materialistic members of the female sex. Someone else whose basic belief is that women are lovely might not even once

have met a woman who is greedy for money. If a woman
believes that she is only loveable if she looks like a model, she
will probably develop an eating disorder and attract men
who criticise her looks even if she is gorgeous in every
respect. This list could go on endlessly, but can be
summarised as follows:

**You attract people on the basis of what you think is
realistic and possible.**

If your past relationships were dissatisfying and you have
put up with misery for years, you might have believed that
you can't expect much else from a man or a woman, that your
partner will change if you only try hard enough, that
you don't have the strength to leave, or that you have to be
'realistic' and stop hanging on to your romantic castles in the
air. It was precisely these negative beliefs that held you for so
long in this painful situation.

If you had truly and completely believed that you are a
gorgeous and loveable person, that you deserve an equally
wonderful partner, that it is a waste of time trying to change
other people, and that it is totally realistic to expect to be
happy and fulfilled on *all* levels with your partner, you
would probably have found a wonderful soulmate long ago
and wouldn't be reading this book.

So, in order to give yourself a chance of finding a really
great partner, you need to let go of any generalised negative ideas about men, women, relationships and yourself.
Instead, you need to allow yourself to believe that there are
at least *some* available gorgeous members of the opposite
sex, and that you are loveable enough to attract the one
that suits you best.

You also need to open up to the possibility that you and
your partner can form an extraordinary relationship that
defies all statistical probability of separation and divorce.
Only if your mind has these 'windows' of positiveness is
there a chance that you will find what you desire.

To Change Negative Beliefs about Men, Women, Relationships and Yourself

- Write on a piece of paper: 'men are...' and complete the sentence as quickly as possible and without thinking a lot.

- Explore other topics in the same way. For example, 'women are..., relationships are..., married people are..., marriage is..., soulmates are..., I am..., someone who looks like me deserves..., someone with my weaknesses deserves...' and so on.

- If you come up with generalised negative ideas (for example, 'soulmate relationships are impossible'), try to argue against them in a way you can believe (for example, 'soulmate relationships are rare and not easy to find but they are not impossible'). Your aim is to at least cut a hole in your negative beliefs that will allow your soulmate to come through one day.

- Write all the positive statements on a piece of paper and keep this in a place where you can look at it from time to time, so that your negative beliefs can't dominate you any more.

The examples in the chart opposite demonstrate how some people have transformed their negative ideas. All these people reported that they felt an immediate sense of relief once they opened up to a more positive possibility.

Note that this is not an exercise in which you replace negative beliefs with positive affirmations you find difficult to believe. If you replace a negative belief like 'men are not trustworthy' with 'men are loving and can be trusted', you might soon feel betrayed again because you were not discerning enough. Your revised belief needs to be rational

Negative Belief	Revised Belief
I am too old to find a partner.	Other people have found partners at my age so it can't be impossible for me either.
There are no good men any more.	I can't be sure about that because I don't know all men. Maybe there are more good men than I realise.
Marriage is boring.	Whether my marriage is boring or not depends on me and my partner. If we are not boring our marriage will not be boring either.
I am just not lucky.	It is the nature of luck that it can change at any time.

and something you can believe easily, like 'some men are untrustworthy, others are very loving, and I need to learn to spot the difference'.

Overcoming Ambivalence

Our own wishes are like seeds that will eventually grow into the most beautiful flowers if they are tended with love and care. If you want to find the partner of your dreams, you first need to have an intention to do so and stick to it, no matter what.

Many people who are single harbour some sort of conscious or unconscious ambivalence about whether to have a new relationship, or stay on their own and become happy 'in themselves'. Being torn in this way means that you sow a seed only to dig it up every so often and replace it with another seed. Unfortunately, nothing much can be achieved in this way; if people don't really know what they want they are loosing time, energy and, most importantly, joy and optimism.

Even someone who has a strong conscious determination to find a partner might feel some ambivalence deep down inside because they fear the many risks that are involved in giving themselves totally to a new love relationship. 'Wouldn't it be nice,' a little voice might whisper in their head, 'to be a happy just with my friends, my work and my family? Then I would be safe and certain to never be heart-broken again.' However, avoiding emotional risks is not the only reason for being ambivalent about finding a partner.

Being alone and unfulfilled could also be a way to show your parents how much they have failed you. 'Look,' you might silently grumble, 'nothing much has come of me because you were such lousy parents.' Your own misery would serve you as a kind of revenge by denying your parents the joy of being proud and happy for you. There are many more reasons for being ambivalent – for example, you may be afraid of loosing your freedom and autonomy, or averse to making compromises with a new partner.

Generally speaking, there is no harm in pursuing your wish for a partner with some nervousness and caution. But if your mind is split into two or more subpersonalities who all want different thing in life, it is as if you are standing on the accelerator and the brake at the same time. In other words, if you can't pursue your wish for a partner whole-heartedly, it will be very difficult for you to find one.

The following exercise is designed to make your possibly unconscious ambivalence conscious and to deal with it skilfully.

To Overcome Ambivalence

- Imagine that you have split into two subpersonalities and that one of them wants a partner and the other doesn't. Arrange two chairs opposite each other and imagine that each of your subpersonalities is sitting on one of the chairs.

- Sit down on one chair and take the place of the subpersonality who wants a partner; look at your 'other half' and explain to it the reasons why you want to have a soulmate.

- Swap chairs and take the place of the subpersonality who wants to stay single; explain why this is so. Just make up something and don't worry that you might decrease your chances of finding a partner if you voice your inner ambivalence. The opposite is true – the more you know how you hinder yourself, the more you can deal with this obstacle skilfully.

- Swap seats again, reply and try to find a compromise.

- Go on swapping seats until you have found a compromise that feels good for both of your sub-personalities.

Note that you can't do this exercise 'just in your mind'. It only works if you get up and move around a bit. The following example shows how Kate discovered that she was much more ambivalent than she knew, and how she resolved her inner conflict.

Kate, subpersonality one: 'I want to have a partner because I want to be loved and to love. It is horrible to always be alone. I want a companion, someone to share my life with.'
Kate, subpersonality two: *Silence*
Ulli: 'Just invent something.'
Kate: 'I can't think of anything, I really want a partner.'
Ulli: 'Just make something up.'
Kate, subpersonality two: 'I am great. I don't need anybody. And anyway, I don't like sex. Men can be like animals and I can't be bothered with all that.'
Kate (shocked): 'That is true, I have some problems with sex but I didn't know it was that bad.'

Ulli: 'Just stay in the dialogue for the time being and we will talk about it later. For now, can you go back to subpersonality one and suggest a compromise?'

Kate, subpersonality one: 'We need to find a man who is really gentle and likes to cuddle without forcing us to have sex all the time.'

Kate, subpersonality two: 'Sounds good, but I am not sure there is such a man.'

Kate, subpersonality one: 'I am sure there is, we just need to make this aspect a priority when we look for someone.'

Kate, subpersonality two: 'Okay, but I will only want to have a partner who takes me sexually as I am, and will not pressurise me in any way.'

Kate, subpersonality one: 'I promise.'

Kate, subpersonality two: 'Okay.' *Smiles*

Kate left the session with renewed confidence because she now understood how she had hindered *herself* by the unconscious fears that she had not dealt with so far.

DEFINE WHAT YOU WANT

Now we come to the actual process of 'sowing the seeds', which is forming and maintaining clear intentions about your dream relationship. People who live with a wonderful soulmate have not just been lucky, even if it looks as though they have from the outside. In reality they have been drawn to each other by their own healthy ideas and high expectations, and their commitment to live by their own high standards. If you want to have a really wonderful relationship you need to do the same, and you mustn't be deterred by the general misery you might perceive in the couples around you. Even if none of your friends believes that it is possible to live in a deeply satisfying relationship, you can prove them all wrong by making up your mind and sticking to your viewpoint, no matter how pessimistic everyone is around you.

Before we get down to business and describe all the desirable attributes of your soulmate, remember that lasting happiness in any relationship only comes from a commitment to love and to grow in love. It is therefore a good idea to start by defining the highest aims of your relationship before turning to things like hair colour and body type.

To Define the Highest Purpose of Your Dream Relationship

- What is the highest purpose of your life? Take your time to mull over this question, because your answer will determine what kind of life you will lead and how much happiness you will experience. Once you know what you want for yourself, you can proceed to define what you wish to be the highest purpose of your dream relationship.

- Write down on a piece of paper what you wish to be the highest purpose of your relationship. What can you as a couple contribute to the world as an expression of your own happiness and fulfilment? For many people one answer is to create a loving space to raise children. Other aims are to take the love and happiness that you have created in your relationship and bring them to the people you work with. Or you might want to create a space with your partner that is a source of inspiration and well-being for all your friends and visitors. You can also think of your highest spiritual aspirations and wish to accomplish them with your partner in order to bring them to the world.

- Decorate your piece of paper in a way that underlines the importance of these high aims, and keep it in a place that is safe and appropriate for the 'seed of your deepest heart-wish'.

- Read through your aims from time to time, and amend them if more or better goals come to mind.

For the second step of sowing the seeds, you have to remember the law of an even deal again. As I have stated before, partners are attracted by the differences in their characters, but they match in their values and what they have to give to each other. A generous woman will not be attracted to a mean man, and an open-minded and explorative man will not be attracted to a woman who is holding back in many ways. In both cases, the giving and taking would be grossly uneven. The law of an even deal states that the more you have to offer, the more you can expect to get from your future dream partner.

Bearing this in mind, in the next step you need to make an honest list of what you have to offer your dream partner, imagining that they will be able to offer you just as much. Note that this is not an exercise in self-improvement, and that you don't have to give any more than you really want to give. As the saying goes, 'there is a lid for every pot', and this exercise is meant to explore your pot. In many of the categories below, you will probably find that you have more to offer than you might have thought. Then you can start looking forwards to your 'matching lid'.

What You Have To Offer Your Dream Partner

Write down what you have to offer your potential dream partner, and include the following areas:

- **Spirituality** Do you want to share prayer and meditation, etc.? Are you tolerant if your partner has different beliefs from yours?

- **Communication** How much and how openly do you want to communicate with your partner? Are you able to restrain aggressive remarks in arguments? How much empathy and sympathy do you have to offer?

- **Affection and closeness** How much are you able to show your loving feelings in words and in deeds? How much do you like to cuddle? How much closeness do you have to offer?

- **Sexuality** How much do you like sex? How willing are you to find out about the needs of your partner and fulfil them?

- **Character** Which parts of your character are appealing? Your humour, warmth, common sense, practicality, sense of adventure, intelligence, sensuality, openness, strength, calmness, vivaciousness, patience, generosity, etc.?

- **Integrity** How honest and trustworthy are you? How much can you be relied on in your promises and agreements?

- **Personal development** How willing are you to work on yourself in order to grow in love and become a more mature person? How willing are you to accept help? How willing are you to give up unhealthy habits? How willing are you to work on the relationship so that both you and your partner will be happier?

- **Commitment** Are you monogamous? Do you want to marry? What kind of commitment do you have to offer your ideal partner?

- **Wealth** How much of your material wealth do you want to share with your partner?

- **Interests** Which of your interests might inspire your partner, and do you want to share them?

- **Education** What kind of education did you have? Are you willing to go on learning through books, courses and other training?

- **Practical support** How willing are you to help your partner with their problems in daily life?

- **Children** Do you want one or more (or none)? How much do you want to care for them?

- **Physical appearance** How do you look? Is grooming, and keeping fit and beautiful, important to you?

- **Location** Do you have a place to live to offer your partner? Would you be able and willing to move?

- **Other relationships** Do you have children or parents to look after, or are you totally free? Would you be willing to give up friends of the opposite sex if your partner wanted this?

- **Health** How is your health? How willing are you to take care of your health and give up unhealthy habits?

- **Power** Do you stand up for your needs? Do you always make sure that you do not dominate your partner?

- **General** How willing are you to regard your partner's well-being to be as important as your own?

When you have completed your offer, read through the list and imagine all the people who would be delighted to have you as a partner. Imagine that they will have as much to give you, and how wonderful your relationship will be. Summarise your list into two or three most important offers. Keep this list in a special place and read through it from time to time. If you feel low in confidence, it will help

you to remember how attractive you are. You can alwa
amend the list if you feel that it is not appropriate any
more.

Concentrating on your offer has many benefits. It will make
you aware of your inner riches, and it will make you more
confident. It will also make you much more attractive to
potential partners, because they will be drawn to someone
who has something to offer rather than to someone who just
feels poor and needy.

There are still more lists you have to write. You obviously
have to write a wish list describing what you are looking for
in your partner. I suggest that you focus first on how you
want to *feel* in your dream relationship. You will have won
nothing if you find a person who is everything you desire,
but makes you feel bad about yourself. If you know how you
want to feel with your partner, it will also be much easier for
you to recognise your soulmate if they don't look exactly as
you imagined they would.

How You Want To Feel with Your Dream Partner

- Write down how you want to feel in yourself in your
  ideal relationship in all of the areas given in the previous
  list. (For example, area **Appearance**: 'I'd like to feel
  beautiful when I am with my partner.' Or, 'I'd like to
  feel physically attracted to my partner.')

- As you write down your feelings, experience and relish
  them right now as deeply as possible.

- Summarise your list into the two or three most
  important feelings you want to experience in your ideal
  relationship.

- Keep this list with your other lists in your special place.
  Read through it from time to time, and try to feel these
  feelings each time as deeply and as clearly as you can.

As examples, people who have done this exercise have come
up with the following:

- **Spirituality** 'I want to feel inspired with my partner and I
  want to feel assured that we have both a similar orientation in our religious beliefs.' Someone else wrote: 'I want
  to feel free and uninhibited to believe whatever I want.'

- **Integrity** 'I want to feel sure that I can trust my partner
  one hundred per cent.'

- **Money** 'I wish to feel safe and well-cared for.' Someone
  else wrote: 'I'd like to feel generous and be confident that
  my partner won't waste any money.'

There is one last list to write, and this of course concerns
what you want in a partner. It is a good idea to be very clear
about what you want in your soulmate in terms of character,
but to be as generous and unspecific as possible when it
comes to details of appearance and possessions. It surely
shouldn't matter too much if the man of your dreams is a
little overweight if he is in other respects the most generous,
sexy, loving and humorous man you can imagine?

In the many years I have counselled single men and
women in finding partners, I have noticed that some men
have surprisingly high expectations about what the woman
of their dreams should look like. They want slim, beautiful
and young women, even if they themselves are advancing in
age, bald and overweight. Worse still, just these men are
often mean with their money, and wouldn't even dream of
sharing it with their future partner. Despite my sometimes
gentle and sometimes brutal confrontations over the fact

that they were ignoring the law of an even deal, these men didn't let go of their unrealistic expectations. Not surprisingly, none of them has yet found a satisfying relationship. In one case, a man found himself a very sexy lady many years younger than himself, but unfortunately she is so immature and neurotic that he can't enjoy the relationship at all. Now he feels sorry for himself, but still doesn't realise that all this is happening precisely in accordance with the law of an even deal.

Women, on the other hand, often make the opposite mistake; they tend not to appreciate what they have to offer, and don't set their goals high enough in terms of finding a man. But according to the law of an even deal, you definitely can expect to get what you are willing to give if your resolutions are honest and if you live by your own standards.

A Wish List for Your Future Partner

- Using the areas of relationships from the exercises above, write down what you would like in your future partner. Keep in mind that you can expect as much as you are willing to give, but not necessarily more.

- Find a few pictures in magazines that symbolise the kind of relationship you desire and stick them around your list.

- Write a summary of the three most important qualities you are looking for in a partner.

- Keep your list and pictures with your other lists in your special place, and look at it as often as you can.

OVERCOMING UNHEALTHY RELATIONSHIP PATTERNS

It is a fact that many people repeat certain negative patterns in relationships; no matter how hard they try, they find it very difficult to get rid of these patterns. Monica, for example, over and over again found herself in relationships with men who were very domineering, while Harry developed a very painful pattern in which he was always drawn to women who liked him as a good friend but not as a sexual partner.

Patterns like this can be difficult to avoid, but once you recognise how you create them yourself you can learn to avoid them once and for all. The only thing you have to learn is to say the difficult little word 'no', and to use it quickly and resolutely each time you recognise that your negative pattern may be repeating itself.

To Overcome Negative Relationship Patterns

- Think of your last relationship, and remember how you felt in each of the different areas described in the previous exercises while you were in the relationship. Note the areas you were most dissatisfied with.

- Analyse all the relationships with your former partners and with your opposite-sex parent in the same way.

- Do you find certain patterns emerging (for example, 'most of my previous partners had problems showing affection,' or, 'my ex-wife as well as my mother were very domineering.')?

- Compare your insights with those you found when you analysed the law of an even deal in your previous relationships (*see page 39*).

- Summarise up to three character traits of your previous partners and your opposite-sex parent that caused you the most trouble in the past, and write them down in an 'avoid list'.

- Make a strong resolution to stay away from people with similar character traits.

In my own life I had to learn to stay away from unloving, untrustworthy men who were prone to addictions. It was really uncanny how often I was approached by just these kinds of men. They answered my lonely-heart adverts, sent me unexpected love letters and approached me at parties. It was as if I had a magnet in my pocket that magically attracted all sorts of liars and addicts.

As time went by, however, I learnt to recognise the early-warning signs more and more quickly, and I was determined to clear my life of these kinds of unfortunate qualities in other people once and for all. As you already know, my efforts were crowned with success, although it took some time and a lot of determination to get to this point.

If you want to stop unhealthy patterns from occurring in your relationships, you have to be equally determined, and you might have to say 'no' many times more than you can imagine. The power to be drawn back into old misery is strong, so you need to be clear and resolute to change your life for the better.

One last word: when you have written all your lists, remember to keep them secret from anyone who might discourage you in your wish for a wonderful soulmate. There are too many pessimistic and 'realistic' people around, and if you want to prove them wrong you need to be a bit secretive.

Chapter 7

Getting Ready

Once you have sown your seeds, you need to create the best circumstances for them to sprout in the shortest time possible. This is done by sprinkling some water over your seeds and then putting a lid on your seed-tray. The lid has two functions: it helps to keep your seeds moist, but even more importantly it creates a mini-greenhouse that keeps your seeds warm by raising the temperature.

What does all this mean for your wish for a soulmate? How can you raise the temperature in your own life and create more energy for your wish for a soulmate to come true?

YOUR GREATEST POWER TO ATTRACT YOUR SOULMATE

When I ask people what could make them more powerful in attracting the partner of their dreams, women sometimes come up with the idea that looking really beautiful would help, and men think that being confident would make all the difference.

Forget about all that! You have much more power than

this, and you can use it even if you are shy and average-looking like most of us are.

The greatest power you have to attract your desired soulmate is your will-power.

In fact, your will-power is the strongest power of all the powers you have. If you really want something and keep striving for it, you will get it one day.

I personally enjoy watching talk-shows with famous people, because many of them are beautiful examples of the saying 'Where there's a will there's a way!' Many celebrities are not particularly attractive in a conventional sense, and some are not even very confident. But I can't help admiring the will-power with which they have made their way to the top.

If you can muster all your will-power and put it behind the aims that *you* find worthwhile, you can get what you want, and will certainly be able to find the love of your life. You don't have to have any special qualities – you just have to want it with all your heart! The following exercise is part of the wish-practice method that you can use to call anything you want into your life. Thousands of people have worked with wish-practice and it has brought about the most wonderful results.

To Dream Your Soulmate Relationship Into Existence

(5 to 10 minutes each day)

- Get comfortable and allow yourself to dream about your desired soulmate relationship. Visualise it in all aspects that are important for you. At the same time, feel all the feelings in yourself that you want to feel once you have found your soulmate. Picture also how you want to live your highest purpose with your partner. Stay in these positive pictures and feelings for five to ten minutes each day until you have found your partner.

- If you find yourself dreaming about a person you know or about someone famous, this will be no problem as long as you do it in the knowledge that you are just using this person as a **model**, and not as a way of imposing your will on them. In particular, if the person you visualise is in a relationship you have to keep your motivation very clear as it would come negatively back to you if you tried to break another couple apart.

- Finish this exercise by saying out loud: 'This wonderful relationship now manifests in my life in the most harmonious way possible for the best of all beings.'

I could give you many examples of people who did the above exercise and found friends, clients and soulmates within a reasonable time-span. In my own life I found a husband who is actually 'better' than I was able to imagine, and I also found the beautiful home, the baby and the self-employed work which were all part of the same visualisation. It seems amazing, but 'just' dreaming and visualising your desired aim over and over again can bring about miracles. If you are particularly interested in this method, you can refer to my book, *Make Your Dreams Come True*.

Staying with your wish and *never* wavering in your intention is one of the most important things that you must do in order to create your wonderful soulmate relationship. Every day you think you'd rather give up on wanting a partner, and every period of time you are undecided about what you want, will be wasted in terms of finding your soulmate. So one of the most important rules is:

Keep up your wish for your soulmate at all times without getting impatient or pushy.

It is very important to hold on to your wish in a relaxed way without getting greedy or angry that it hasn't come true yet. Just know what you want and try to be undeterred by the pessimism around you, and by your own lack of trust. Instead, think about something you have wished for whole-heartedly and which you have achieved. This can be something as simple as wanting to pass your school exams or finding a suitable home. In the same way, you can find your soulmate.

If you are like most people, you will go through phases when you will be more confident and optimistic about finding your partner soon, and there will be times when you will loose all hope and despair at the seemingly appalling lack of suitable partners. These mood swings are totally natural, but it is important to learn not to drown in resignation after every unsuccessful blind date.

In the following exercise you can make use of symbol therapy. This has been successfully used by many people to maintain trust and hope in times when their life hasn't given them any signs that their partner is around the next corner.

To Maintain Trust in Finding Your Soulmate

- Relax in way that is convenient to you.

- You are now ready to come into contact with your Higher Consciousness, who will help you to overcome your lack of trust. See your Higher Consciousness as an angelic being surrounded by light, or as a beautiful shimmering light that has a living and loving quality. Feel how you are embraced by the love and support of your Higher Consciousness.

- Ask your Higher Consciousness: 'Can you please give me a healing symbol to overcome my suffering, which comes from not trusting that I will find my soulmate soon, for the best of all beings?'

- You might be shown one or several symbols (for example flowers, gems or geometrical forms), and you should pick one that you find attractive and that has a beautiful and bright colour. Acknowledge the very first thought or idea of a symbol that comes into your mind. If you are not sure whether you have received the right symbol, you can check with your Higher Consciousness. Watch for an inner feeling of 'yes' or 'no'.

- When you have received a healing symbol you feel good about, thank your Higher Consciousness for its help.

- Say to yourself, 'I always love myself deeply with all my weaknesses, and even if I can't trust that I will find my soulmate soon.'

- Visualise your healing symbol in the middle of your chest in your heart, and when you breathe out exhale the colour of your symbol throughout your body, into the area surrounding your body and into your world. Do this in the most loving way possible. When you breathe in, just enjoy the presence of your symbol in your heart. Then exhale the colour and the positive qualities of your symbol again. Do this in a loving way for two minutes. Then open your eyes again.

- Work with your healing symbol in this way for two minutes a day and whenever you start to worry that your wish will not come true. Always start by saying, 'I always love myself deeply with all my weaknesses and even if I can't trust that my wish will come true.' Visualise your symbol in exactly the form it was given to you by your Higher Consciousness and never change it yourself. If it seems to change of its own accord, don't allow this to happen but always go back to its original form.

THE GREATEST HELP IN FINDING YOUR SOULMATE

The greatest power in finding your soulmate that is available in the universe is your Higher Consciousness. It is totally up to you by what name you call it, or if you simply see it as the part of your mind that is more loving and wise than your everyday consciousness. Your Higher Consciousness is the greatest power in the universe because it is the source of all love and all wisdom that exists.

You don't have to be a deeply spiritual person to make contact with your Higher Consciousness. All you need to do is to open up to the possibility that there is much more love and wisdom available than you can see with your ordinary eyes. Our Higher Consciousness is the essence of our being and resides in the depth of our loving heart, yet it is outside of us and we share it with every single being in the universe.

When we are able to bring together our own will-power and combine it with deep surrender to our Higher Consciousness, we can achieve incredible things. This is what Jesus meant when he said, 'Faith can move mountains.' Our Higher Consciousness can't give or withhold things from us in a random way. If this were the case, He would be a very cruel god. The truth is, whether we suffer or are happy, we are in charge of our own destiny. However, our Higher Consciousness can help us tremendously if our aims are in alignment with its love and wisdom. So, anything we want that will create more love for ourselves and others will be strongly supported by the highest powers of this universe. Therefore when you visualise your dream relationship, include a little prayer in which you ask for the help and support of your Higher Consciousness.

I have never met anyone who has prayed sincerely for a soulmate while letting go of all old hurts and addictions who didn't find someone within a reasonable time-span. It can't be any other way! If you have cleared negativity from your life and want to find love with all your heart while surrendering deeply to the power of your Higher Consciousness, you have brought yourself to the highest energy level possible. It will not be long before you can embrace the love of your life.

BECOMING MORE ATTRACTIVE

What is the most attractive quality in a real soulmate? It is certainly not outstanding beauty, although some people might be tempted to believe that this is the case because we live in a society that worships beauty and youth to an extent that verges on the obsessive.

We are told to believe that the younger and more beautiful we look, the greater are our chances on the partner-market. However, like any market, the partner-market works according to the law of an even deal, and many scientific studies have shown that when it comes to physical appearance, people match up roughly according to their level of attractiveness. In other words, when you look average you have the biggest choice for the simple reason that there are more people in the average category than in any other.

Despite widely held beliefs, stunningly beautiful people do not have the best chances of finding a real life-partner, no matter how much they are desired and admired for their looks. On the contrary, less attractive people (who outnumber them greatly) usually don't go near them for fear of being rejected, and out of fear of never being able to feel comfortable with someone who is so much more attractive than themselves.

In my counselling practice I have made the interesting observation that the more beautiful a woman looks the more often she complains that her partner criticises her appearance. On the other hand, I have hardly ever heard someone with average looks say that they have had a similar hurtful

experience. Why would that be? Why are women more criticised for their appearance the better they look? The answer
can only be found by understanding the law of an even deal.

A stunningly beautiful woman can be a challenge for the
confidence of her partner because he might wonder whether
he has enough to offer to her. He may even be afraid that
she might run off with a 'better' man. And what does he do
if he is not very conscious and mature? He criticises her
appearance in order to destroy some of her confidence, and
in this way limits the risk that she might think she 'deserves'
more than he can offer her. In other words, he tries to make
his partner believe that the deal between them is fair and
that she is lucky to have found him. Unfortunately, this tactic
often works quite well if the woman is not very confident in
the first place. (By the way, some women do equally nasty
things to their men in areas where it hurts him the most.)

I can therefore assure those who believe that they must
look like film stars in order to find a partner that nothing
could be further from the truth.

But we still haven't solved the question of what makes
people more attractive to a potential partner.

**There is nothing more attractive than people who are at
ease with themselves.**

And there is nothing less attractive than people who hate
themselves, indulge in their addictions and find it impossible
to bear their own company, so that they greedily grasp at
anyone who might be able to rescue them from themselves.
Conversely, if someone radiates inner harmony and beauty,
a lot of people will feel attracted to them.

So the first and foremost thing you have to do in order to
become more attractive is to love yourself and to become
your own best friend. Can you imagine completely stopping
criticising yourself, never scolding yourself or never making
ridiculing remarks about yourself? Can you imagine all your
thoughts about yourself being warm and well-meaning? If

you can stop being hard on yourself, you will be surprised how easy it is to give up bad habits and to genuinely be more relaxed and happy.

Loving yourself is a skill that can be learnt, like roller-skating or typewriting. This means that you need a bit of discipline at the beginning and after that it will become second nature.

To Learn to Love Yourself

- Remember how it feels to love someone by recalling a situation in which you felt great love (not desire!) for someone. Loving someone means really wishing the best for them, like a parent does naturally for their baby.

- Without changing this feeling or thinking a lot, turn this love to yourself and envelope yourself in a cloud of warm and loving feelings.

- Direct this love to all the aspects of your character and body that you like, and equally to all the aspects of your personality and body that you dislike. Remember, everything changes best under the influence of love and, conversely, becomes rigid under the influence of dislike.

- Talk to yourself about your wishes and problems in a loving and well-meaning way, as a loving parent would talk to their only child.

- Repeat this exercise often, and in particular when you feel low and lonely.

It is interesting to compare a loving attitude to yourself that will enhance your attractiveness, with a self-assured attitude of 'I think I'm great' that will actually *decrease* your attractiveness. The reasons for this surprising dynamic are again found in understanding the law of an even deal. Remember, others are only attracted to us if we can give them what they want to have. But equally, a potential partner needs to sense that we desire what they have to offer, too. Otherwise they would feel superfluous. We all want to be loved, but we also want to feel that our partner needs us.

So, if someone thinks he is 'great', it is as if he is saying 'I don't particularly need you – I am wonderful already.' There would not be much for a potential partner to give this person, and no deficiency to be filled. Anyone who might feel initially attracted to such a person would become very frustrated by the lack of exchange between them as time went by. On the other hand, when you love yourself you are not saying that you are perfect. You love yourself *with* all your weaknesses and deficiencies, and therefore you will be desirable for your inner beauty as well as for what you need.

BECOMING EVEN MORE ATTRACTIVE

There is only one thing that is more attractive than people who are at ease with themselves, and that is people who are at ease with themselves *and* caring towards others at the same time. Imagine someone who moves with grace and confidence and spills over with humour, someone who can enjoy the pleasures of life without a bad conscience, but also knows their limits and when to say 'no'. And now imagine this person has warm and loving eyes and a genuine interest in the well-being of the people around them. Wouldn't they be highly attractive?

Everyone can become like this. It's not that difficult, and loving yourself is the first step. As a general rule, everyone treats others in roughly the same way that they treat themselves, and the more someone loves themselves the more natural it will be for them to extend this love to others. And according to the law of an even deal, this love will come back naturally and effortlessly sooner or later.

The most attractive people love themselves and others as well.

The Dalai Lama teaches a wonderful little meditation that 'trains' the ability to love yourself and others in equal measure; this can be practised anywhere you are.

To Practise Loving Yourself and Others

- Remember that everyone is the same in that we all want to be loved and happy.

- When you breathe in send love to yourself.

- When you breathe out send love to others, whether you like them or not. Just wish that everyone can find true happiness (and at the same time become much more likeable as well).

- Do this little exercise as often as you can and marvel at the transformation it will bring to your mood and finally to your whole life.

In order to be really attractive, you can't afford to allow your radiance to be spoiled by negative and hateful thoughts about yourself and others. If you still harbour some well-cared-for negative attitudes about the opposite sex in general, now is the time to finally let them go. Your wish for a soulmate will prosper best if your mind is positive and loving. With this emotional attitude you are most likely to meet someone who defies everything negative you have ever assumed about men, women or yourself.

If you want a real soulmate it is important for you to make

a dedication to grow in love now, even if you are still on your own. This will usually involve a path of self-development, prayer, meditation or healing. In this way, you will be able to unravel your potential to be a truly loving person, and you will find it so much easier to attract the person of your dreams.

Making Contact with Your Future Partner

There is one particular practice that will help you to become more confident and attractive, and that is making contact with your future partner. Even if this seems like a strange idea, it is actually possible to speak to your future soulmate right now, as if you were phoning them on your mobile phone.

Do we really know how mobile phones work and how it is possible to send little waves through the air to talk to someone else? I don't, but like everyone else, I trust that the system works. If someone had told people a hundred years ago that we would soon all talk into little wireless boxes in order to communicate with each other, they would have laughed. As we now know, they would have been wrong to laugh. It is not laughable, either, to consider sending messages through the ether just with your mind similarly to the way you use your mobile phone.

Even if you can't quite believe what I am suggesting, the following exercise is wonderful for connecting you with your inner riches and will raise your trust in finding your soulmate soon.

To Make Contact with Your Future Soulmate

• Imagine that your future soulmate exists somewhere and is longing for you just as much as you are longing for them. See or feel this person in your mind without being too specific about hair colour and body type; instead try to sense their character and inner beauty.

- Feel love in your heart welling up as you think about this lovely and desirable person.

- Start to talk to your future soulmate and tell them about all the things you want to share. Rejoice with delight as you listen to the responses of your future partner – as you find that they like everything that is important to you, and that they look forward to sharing it with you.

- Listen to what your future partner has to offer you and tell them how much you look forward to your first 'real' meeting.

- Talk about your dreams and worries, and feel how only love and understanding come back.

Practise this inner communication as often and as long as you like, and remember that it is not a fantasy or an escape from reality. This exercise is meant to create and strengthen the spiritual connection with a real person who you can meet if you follow the rest of the steps in Part II of this book.

You can even go one step further and buy a little present for your future soulmate, or write them a Valentine's Day card. (Don't worry that people might think you've gone mad. Just don't tell anyone about your activities and enjoy the fact that you are connecting with the deeper working of the universe.)

One word of warning: note that this exercise is not meant to motivate a married colleague to split up from his wife and propose to you. That wouldn't be ethical. You can use the inner image of a married person you know only as a *model*. Generally speaking, it is not a good idea to be too specific in the way you picture your future soulmate, because that might cause you to become too fixated on certain aspects of appearance, which would be an obstacle to finding someone in 'real life'. Instead, focus on the love and joy this exercise evokes in you. Relish the increased trust in you that your soulmate really exists and that you only have to meet each other. In the next chapter you can find out how to go about this.

Chapter 8

Meeting Potential Partners

After all the work of getting the seed-trays ready, and the excitement of sowing the seeds and creating more energy, we are now coming to the daily nitty-gritty of finding a partner, which means going on dates. When you are young this is usually easier than when you are older, because the whole world is like a big introductory service full of people of your age who want to find a partner. But people who are advancing in age rarely have a social life or work environment where they can meet single people of the opposite sex on a regular basis.

Most men and women who are approaching middle age and beyond need to actively create opportunities to meet someone who is desirable and available. In other words, if you are a bit older and you really want a partner, it is simply not enough to insist that everything should go the 'natural way' while living a life in which you hardly ever meet new people. Instead, you need to get up and go out of your way to find the love of your life.

This engagement is very beneficial, if for no other reason than because it gets your energy going and gives your Higher Consciousness a sign that you are serious about your desire. You might even find that after months of going on blind dates, you will finally be able to pluck up your courage and approach your neighbour, who you have fancied for years. In this case, your search activities were necessary for building up your confidence with the other sex, and to help you to develop enough insight to finally approach what was always in front of your nose.

Dating is important because it is a good way of learning more about your needs and wishes. It also gives you an opportunity to make platonic friends, which is extremely beneficial because it helps you learn more about how members of the other sex tick. With a platonic friend of the opposite sex, you can talk about all the things that never worked out in your past relationships and ask them for their opinion on why this was so. In all likelihood, you will get very different answers from those that you got when you talked to your same-sex friends.

Having platonic friends also provides you with the precious opportunity to give love and appreciation to members of the opposite sex. The law of an even deal works in intricate and invisible ways, but basically it is like a bank account and the more you pay in the more you get out. This means that the more you get used to the idea of being loving towards members of the opposite sex, the better chance you will have of attracting a soulmate into your life.

Going on dates can also provide you with good feedback about how much you are still ruled by old bitterness, fear and an uncaring attitude, which can resurface when you meet someone who reminds you of something negative you experienced in the past. If you can go on a blind date with a caring and friendly attitude and maintain positive feelings even if it turns out that your date doesn't meet any of your standards, you are well on the way to finding someone who really matches your maturity.

WHERE CAN YOU FIND POTENTIAL PARTNERS?

The best places to find a partner are venues where people meet who have similar values to yours. As already discussed, your deepest ideals are at the heart of every relationship and will finally determine whether your partnership will be a happy one. In this respect, spiritual people have a clear advantage because they can always meet like-minded people at their place of worship. Singles clubs, on the other hand, bring together a multitude of different people who have only one thing in common, which is wanting to find a partner. This is simply not enough, and it is very unlikely that you will be able to find a real soulmate in such a place.

It is a good idea to take out your wish lists for your dream partner and to brainstorm where such a person might go. You can also ask trustworthy friends about their ideas. As a general rule, it is always best to try to meet someone in places where you would go repeatedly, like in an evening class that lasts several weeks, or on an organised holiday of some kind. Most relationships need a little bit of time to grow, and if you meet for only one evening or one weekend, you may not even notice how attractive someone is, let alone find the opportunity to ask for telephone numbers, and so on.

It is important to only go to meetings and classes that genuinely interest you. Imagine how terrible you would feel if you spent a lot of money and used your precious summer holiday to go on a mountain-climbing course, and all the men on the course were deadly boring and you hated sport anyway.

Another way of meeting potential partners is to arrange blind dates through lonely-hearts columns, Internet-dating or dinner clubs. There is nothing shameful or dangerous in this. On the contrary, working for your wish in this direct way is a sign that you are taking care of yourself and showing your Higher Consciousness your willingness to cooperate in the fulfilment of your wish. Blind dates can, however, be emotionally draining, because people often build up huge expectations when contacting someone. When they finally meet them they often know within seconds that the man or woman is not for them. But then they still have to spend the evening in the company of their date out of politeness.

In order to avoid such disappointments, you need to make your advert as specific as possible. It is no use saying something like, 'I am female with a good sense of humour and I like cinemas and eating out', because this description would fit at least ninety per cent of all women. Instead, write about your deepest heart-wishes and values, and about the highest purpose of your dream relationship. Don't worry that you advert will stand out, because this is exactly what you want it to do. You will be surprised at how different the responses will be, and at how many more suitable partners will reply.

THE FIRST STEPS IN A RELATIONSHIP ARE DECISIVE

If you could examine the inside of a seed-grain, you would find that it contains the complete information about the whole plant in all its intricate forms and life phases. In the same way, the whole of a relationship is contained in the first few early encounters of two partners, just as the first few steps of a dance determine whether it will be a tango or a waltz. Like a seed, every beginning of a long-term process contains the entire information about what is likely to happen in the future. In other words, as a relationship begins, so it is likely to continue.

Some people find this difficult to believe and say that they only knew years later what a 'bad character' their ex-partner had. But I say that if they had had their eyes open, they could have noticed some early-warning signs in their first two encounters with their ex-partner. These signs are there as surely as there is DNA in a seed-grain that can identify the plant that will emerge from it.

The first two encounters between two people contain all the information about their future relationship.

Let me give you an example. A client of mine complained that her boyfriend was unable to commit to her. When we analysed her first two encounters with him, it turned out that she herself had arranged these meetings (in other words, she had done too much for him without waiting for a come-back from him), and that he had told her (among many flattering compliments) that he was unable to fall in love with any woman. Apart from that they saw each other all the time and had a passionate sex life, which made my client believe that they were each other's 'love of their life'. When I pointed out to her that he had clearly told her about his inability to love and commit, she argued ferociously against it because she just didn't want to face up to the truth.

In other cases, the early-warning signs might be less obvious, and some people find it surprising that little things like white lies, a bit of meanness or being late can really mean that much. You can find out for yourself if what I say is true.

Think of one of your ex-partners and remember both their most difficult and their most beautiful character traits. Now think back to your first two encounters with them and try to detect traces of both these qualities. In all likelihood it will be quite easy to remember their beautiful parts, because you probably fell in love with them. But in most cases, you will also see that an angry person was already evident then in a small display of anger, or that an overly dependent person displayed some signs of this characteristic even then. In some cases, you may find that you just had an inexplicable negative feeling that turned out to be justified later on.

What does all this mean for your dating? First of all, it should encourage you to watch out for the early-warning signs. This is particularly true if you are the sort of person who is very loving and trusting, and if you just can't believe that not everyone is like yourself.

It is interesting that the ability to see another person very clearly, with all their positive and negative aspects, is particularly strong when you've just got to know each other. But once two people are falling in love, and in particular when they have started to have sex, their ability to see each other clearly decreases more and more. This process is described well in the sayings, 'Love makes you blind', and 'People who are in love are wearing rose-coloured spectacles'. Quite a few people have had the experience of waking up with a shock from a passionate love affair, when it has dawned on them that they have formed a deep relationship with someone who has great deficiencies in their character.

Why is our ability to see someone clearly stronger at the beginning of a relationship, and why does it decrease as the partnership becomes more intimate? The answer can be found by looking at the unavoidable merging process that happens between two people who are close to each other.

When we strongly desire someone, we don't want to see anything that could function as a barrier between us, and when we finally unite with the object of our desire we literally loose sight. Through sexual and emotional intimacy, we partly merge with another person. In this process we lose a piece of our former identity and take on bits of the energy of our partner. This is exactly the moment when we can't see our partner clearly any more from 'our' point of view – a trend that increases as our relationship becomes closer and closer.

The only protection against the possible negative results of this 'honeymoon blindness' is to have your eyes and ears wide open *before* you fall deeply in love, and *before* you start a sexual relationship. Only then can you be sure that you still have your full ability to see someone clearly, and it is important to take as much time as possible for this phase.

Understanding people's character and seeing the early-warning signs is not always easy, and in Chapter 10 you will find more information on this subject. For the moment, let's look at what it means for you that the first two meetings of a new relationship contain all the information for its future.

First of all, you need to make sure that you implement the law of an even deal *from the very beginning*. In particular, women have to be very careful not to ignore this law. They might think it is a sign of self-confidence and love if they pursue a man without carefully waiting for a come-back, but in reality they will only be destroying the sensitive balance of an even deal that is the only guarantee for lasting happiness.

Men, on the other hand, have to take good care not to be too passive. No matter how emancipated women may appear on the surface, deep down many of them want to be taken care of by a strong and confident man. So if you expect women to make most of the moves towards you, many of them will quickly lose interest.

Implementing the law of an even deal means having equal giving and taking from the very beginning.

Most men and women gain even more romantic fulfilment if the man gives a little bit more, while the woman 'pays him back' by appreciating his efforts. On a practical level, this means that if you are a man you should make one or two moves towards her and then check if she likes this. If you are a woman, make no more than one move towards him and then wait to see if he comes towards you. This waiting can be hard if you are otherwise a confident and strong person, but if you want to have a romantic relationship with an equally strong man you really should take this rule to heart.

There are two more things you have to be aware of at the very beginning of a relationship. Firstly, there is a great deal of lying involved in the blind-dating scene. People lie about their age, about their achievements and about almost everything in order to lure someone from the opposite sex to meet them in person. However understandable these lies are, they are not a good idea because a lie will always leave a bitter and untrustworthy streak in a relationship, even if it survives the initial frustration of the person who has been lied to. Secondly, it is not advisable to date a person who is already in a committed relationship because the pain you would inflict on the person you betray would come back to you sooner or later. Many times I have talked to clients who have cheated on others, and I have always found that they carried strong guilt feelings around with them that prevented them from fully enjoying their new partner.

These dynamics have nothing to do with moral prescriptions or even with punishment from God. They are simply the result of the working of the law of an even deal, which says that we always get back what we give out.

In order to build the best foundations for any relationship, arrive on a blind date as your best but true self, leave old sorrows and problems at home, and implement the law of an even deal from the very beginning. Even if your date is not exactly what you wished for, try to be as positive and friendly as possible. In case you strike lucky, you have planted a pure and healthy seed that can flower into the most exquisite soulmate relationship.

Do You Want Romance?

If you are one of those people who don't care a lot about romantic fulfilment, including candle-light, red roses and romantic presents, you can skip the following section. But if you *do* love romance, now is the moment to give up all your remaining ideas that men and women should somehow always be the same. Romantic fulfilment can only thrive on the condition that two people relish their gender identity to the extent where a woman becomes even more feminine and a man becomes even more masculine. Then their heightened magnetic attraction can pull them together in the most delightful and erotic way.

Because the first two encounters in a relationship are so essential, it is crucial to establish the romantic dimension from the very beginning. This is because it will be hard to change these patterns once a relationship has started on the wrong footing. The beginning of a relationship is literally like the first steps in a dance. It will determine whether you dance in a romantic and erotic way, or are like brother and sister who argue straight away about who is the leader and whether one of you has trodden on the toes of the other.

As I said before, the law of an even deal applies to these first two encounters as much as it applies to the whole relationship, and men and women have to give to each other in equal measures to develop a mutually satisfying relationship. However, in order to find romantic fulfilment they should not always give and take exactly the same things, but have a kind of 'work division' where men do more of the pursuing, while women 'pay' him back by being appreciative and grateful. It is this – admittedly old-fashioned – recipe that will invariably satisfy the deepest romantic desires of most men, as well as those of most women.

For her

Dos

- First of all, develop a good sense of your own preciousness. You are like a beautiful flower and there will be someone out there who will love you just for what you are.

- Stay in your feminine side, and see yourself like a beautiful flower who attracts others through her enticing magnetism. You don't have to do a lot, and you can leave most of the pursuing to the man.

- If you try to find a partner through adverts, it should be you who advertises and he who answers, so that you can stay in your feminine receptive side.

- Let him make most of the moves towards you but smile encouragingly, tell him what you appreciate about him and make inviting comments like, 'This was a *really* lovely evening.' Many men have been bruised by criticism of their masculinity and they often need a lot of encouragement to take the male role.

- For every move he makes towards you and for every bit of gallantry, express your appreciation and gratefulness.

- You can make *half* of the moves towards him (but no more), and you are not condemned to sit at the telephone in a waiting position. But be very careful not to do more than he does. Remember, men and women experience most romantic fulfilment if the man does a little bit more for the woman, and if the woman gracefully appreciates his efforts. If a man is too passive to make most of the moves, decide whether you want to pursue the relationship. If you don't, let him go.

- Focus on how *you* feel in these first encounters. Do you feel beautiful, interesting and talented? Do you feel supported and cared for? If the answer is yes, you are on the right track.

- Pay attention to the warning signs. Does anything make you feel uncomfortable? Does he let you wait? Does he boast, tell any lies or drink too much?

- Find out about him in a light-hearted and appreciative way, so that he doesn't feel as though he is being interrogated.

Don'ts

- If you want romance avoid being in your masculine side, and don't pursue the man of your dreams as if you are a man yourself.

- Avoid making most moves towards him. Invite, encourage and appreciate, but let him make most decisive steps towards you.

- When you try to find a partner through adverts, don't answer his adverts because that would put you in the role of the male pursuer.

- Don't give him the message that you can manage very well without a man, because that would deny him the masculine role of a hero and caretaker.

- Don't talk about your biggest problems and shortcomings. At the moment he wants to be your knight, but not necessarily your therapist. Talking about problems will come later.

- Don't interrogate him, because that would put him into the feminine receptive role and it doesn't feel nice anyway.

- Don't do too much for him, because if you do you will not find out what would come to you voluntarily from him.

- Don't be lured into the masculine active role if he is passive and slow. You might get more contact, but you will find less romantic fulfilment.

- Don't feel obliged to pay him back for everything that he gives you. If he pays for a meal, you are by no means obliged to kiss him or to do even more. A smile and a warm thank you is more than enough.

For him

Dos

- First of all, get a good sense of your strength and your inner goodness. You have something to give and there will be an attractive woman out there who will deeply appreciate it.

- Be brave and take the risk of making most of the moves towards her. You may get the odd rejection, but that should not deter you. Remember, women love courageous men and your chances with any woman will rise merely because you were brave enough to approach her.

- Focus on what you can do to please her. If you can make her happy, you will be happy as well.

- Ask interested questions and listen to her. She will greatly appreciate your caring attitude.

- If you like her, phone her one or two days after your date and tell her that you would like to see her again. There is no danger of appearing too eager. On the contrary, if she likes you she will be delighted, and if she doesn't you will be able to move on more quickly.

- Pay for the drinks! Although this advice might seem unfair at a time when women can earn as much as men, paying for the drinks will give out a strong message that you care. If a woman desires romance and you can't even pay for the drinks, she will probably not want to see you again.

Don'ts

- Don't wait until she initiates or asks for your next meeting. Instead, take the risk of making most of the moves towards her. If she likes you, your courage will be rewarded with much more romantic fulfilment.

- Don't be mean. The more you can please her and do for her, the greater your chances for romance now and later on.

- Don't feel obliged to keep giving if she doesn't appreciate your efforts. Romance can only thrive with a receptive and appreciative woman, and she will show you from the very beginning if she is like this.

- Don't talk about your bigger problems, or complain about how you were rejected by other women in your past. At this time, a woman is more interested in your strengths.

- Don't try to impress her with your achievements. She will be much more impressed by your humility and your caring attitude.

- Don't talk all the time. Instead ask her questions and listen sympathetically.

- Don't necessarily give up if you receive a 'no'. It might come from a misunderstanding, and if you really like the woman it is worth asking her at least one more time.

Chapter 9

Being Playful and Patient

Maybe one day someone will invent a method of finding a soulmate instantly. You would just switch on your computer, type in your details and find your perfect match within seconds. Unfortunately, this method has not been invented yet, and these days it can take a little longer. I won't lie to you: if you want to find the truly satisfying, deeply enjoyable love of your life it can take years. It might go more quickly if you are lucky, but in many cases there will be some waiting time involved before you can finally embrace your true soulmate.

The waiting time doesn't need to be a disaster. On the contrary, it is best viewed as a preparation time in which you can get ready for your final destination. You can compare it with going to university in order to become a doctor. No matter how much a young person desires to be a successful surgeon, they still have to go through some studying before they are finally allowed to hold the knife. In the same way, most people have to learn to develop more happiness and contentment in themselves in order to find a deeply fulfilling relationship.

Learning to be more fulfilled when your wish for a partner

has not yet come true can be a challenge, and for many people this process can take time. However, the more genuine happiness you have found in yourself, the more you can expect to find a partner who is on the same level, and the more fulfilling your relationship will be.

The most important ingredients for achieving this happiness are developing more love for yourself as well as for others, topics that were dealt with in Chapter 7. However, even if someone is wonderfully loving they will still not be happy as long as they haven't put one more ingredient into the mixture. This ingredient is patience.

Let me put it this way: as long as we crave a partner madly and obsessively, we will attract people who will either take advantage of our neediness or are as obsessed as we are. Unfortunately, their obsession might not be for us, but for food, alcohol or sex with many different partners. This sad dynamic cannot be avoided because we always match our partner in our level of maturity, and a relationship between two very needy and obsessed people will invariably be unhappy.

On the other hand, if people let go of their wish for a partner altogether because they don't want to feel the frustration any longer, nothing much is achieved either. In order to fulfil our dreams we need to maintain the desire to do so. If someone says, 'I don't care any more whether I find a partner or not' and really means it, it's like closing the case. It would be extremely unlikely for someone with such an attitude to find a truly awesome life-partner.

The trick is to maintain your wish for a soulmate whole-heartedly, while letting go of your impatience and frustration because you haven't found them yet.

Spending some time by yourself before you start a new relationship can be a real blessing, because it gives you a chance to grow and to develop, so that your next relationship will definitely be better and more fulfilling.

I know quite a few women who are going from one partner to the next in a never-ending line of unhappy and frustrating relationships. When I was much younger and single myself, I sometimes marvelled at their ability to find new boyfriends so quickly – often it was only weeks after the break-up of one relationship before they were in a new, committed relationship again. However, twenty years on I can see that it is much easier to find a partner – any partner – than to have the determination and stamina to wait for the one who it was worth waiting for.

None of these women gave herself the time to reformulate her expectations and to stick to her new aims. They were much too desperate to find someone to rescue them from their loneliness, and they almost threw themselves at the feet of nearly everyone who happened to cross their path.

For many women, one of the most important lessons is to develop the attitude of, 'I will either find a truly satisfying relationship or remain alone.'

Once women have developed this inner strength while letting go of all their old resentments, it is usually only a short time before they find a really wonderful man.

For men, the big challenge is to avoid relationships in which they are only half-heartedly engaged. For one thing, the man may be breaking the heart of the woman he goes out with, who might believe that the relationship means much more to him than he is willing to admit. For another reason, he will not be free to find a *real* soulmate even if he thinks he is. A soulmate relationship could never flourish on the heartache of a person who has been abandoned for the sake of it, just as our beautiful flower could never prosper on poisoned soil.

One of the most important lessons for many men is to learn to regard other people's well-being to be as important as their own.

Once they can do this whole-heartedly and consistently, it will only be a matter of time before they find a really wonderful woman.

I know from my own experience that it can be hard to be on your own and to be patient when you deeply long for a partner. The next sections show you how to achieve some equanimity even if it takes a little bit of time to find your soulmate.

ENJOYING THE PROCESS OF LOOKING FOR A PARTNER

One of the most important things to do while looking for your soulmate is to learn to enjoy the process. Despite all the possible frustrations of being single, looking for a soulmate can also be a great time of exploration, having fun and playfully trying things out. The more you can approach finding a soulmate in a playful way, the easier it will be to finally find your dream partner.

If people deny themselves the joys that they can have while they are single, they are in danger of becoming uptight and bitter. For example, if a woman doesn't allow herself all sorts of contacts with men because she is *only* interested in meeting her soulmate, she will probably feel more lonely than a woman who allows herself to flirt and to have fun with men as much as she can. The second kind of woman will not only enjoy herself more, but she will also be more attractive because of the beauty of her fun-loving attitude.

On the other hand, if a man or woman looks at a potential partner with only one question in mind – 'Is this the one?' – this creates a lot of pressure and might deter people. Too much neediness is not attractive, because no one likes to be 'caught' or even devoured by someone who is desperate. Giving someone the impression that you are *just* playing around is not very attractive either. The most desirable people are those who clearly express their wish for a partner while remaining relaxed and happy.

Having fun with potential partners means flirting, talking and having as much eroticism as feels right for both people. It is, however, important to avoid being trapped in better-than-nothing relationships that don't bring real satisfaction while obstructing the possibility of finding a real soulmate. Let me put it this way: the more someone is at ease with the opposite sex and the more they are able to enjoy flirting and being close to each other, the easier it will be for them to relate to the person who will finally be 'the one'.

Being playful in the process of trying to find a partner also means developing some humour about the many peculiar things you can encounter on the 'dating-scene'. If you get too depressed or angry about the numerous conceited men and demanding women you meet you will only develop a bitter streak, and this will not be good for your attractive-ness. It is better to be able to laugh about the many ways people try to attract a mate while desperately trying to protect themselves.

Learning something in the process

Besides focusing on having fun, it is also a good idea to keep an eye on what you can learn through your different experi-ences. Every time you meet a potential partner you can learn something about yourself, your wishes and the opposite sex, and this will help you to be clearer about what you want and don't want. At the end of the day, the happiness of your future relationship will more or less depend on the wisdom of your choice of a partner; so the more you can learn now the wiser your choice will be and the more happiness you can expect.

Whenever you meet someone who is not right for you, try to pinpoint exactly what you liked in them and what disturbed you about them. You can then use this analysis to reaffirm what you are looking for in your dream partner.

Doing this is not meant to make you overly critical, and you certainly should never tell your date about your thoughts. Instead, these questions are meant to sharpen your awareness about what is important to you to enable you to find real happiness.

As I have said before, many people don't really know what will bring them true happiness and they blindly follow their vague ideas without ever properly investigating them. Meeting lots of potential partners will give you the invaluable possibility of investigating more and more deeply what you are really looking for in a man or a woman apart from good looks, humour and warmth.

The way you choose your dates can also provide you with important feedback about the types of people you feel drawn to. If, for example, you often unconsciously answer lonely-hearts adverts of people who have character traits that are familiar but difficult for you, this is a warning sign that you are still in danger of being sucked into your old negative patterns. In this case, you need to make a strong resolution to recognise when you are on the wrong track more quickly, and to learn to attract different kinds of people.

Going on blind dates can sometimes be emotionally exhausting, but if you keep in mind your aim to learn something from every encounter, no blind date will ever be a waste of time. On the contrary, you will always be able to use these meetings to improve your knowledge of what a real soulmate relationship is about. As you gain more clarity, you will move closer to the person who is destined for you.

DEALING WITH LONELINESS

Some single people feel more lonely than others, and the strength of this negative feeling depends on three factors. How much love and support you can:

1. Give yourself.

2. Feel from your Higher Consciousness.

3. Get from friends and family.

Being your own best friend

Being alone and lonely can be tough, but it can also be the doorway through which we have to go to find more happiness than we ever imagined is possible.

We can most easily change the way we relate to ourselves when we are on our own, and our relationship with ourselves will determine how all our other personal relationships will be.

If we are very self-critical, for example, we will find it hard to develop warm and loving relationships with others because our critical attitude might disturb the people around us. But if we are too self-assured and assume that most people are inferior to us, we will also find it difficult to develop the types of relationship that bring real happiness. Only if we can relate to ourselves like a loving and trustworthy friend will our relationships with others develop in the same satisfying way.

Imagine that you could relate to yourself as if you were your best friend for twenty-four hours a day. Wouldn't that be nice? It would mean that you would *never* criticise yourself any more, and that you would always talk to yourself in a loving and appreciative way. Friends don't say nasty things to you like, 'Oh my god, you are so fat,' or, 'Look at yourself; you will never amount to anything.' They are kind to each other, and if they really feel they need to give a piece of good advice, they try to do so as kindly and constructively as possible. As your own best friend, you would be able to do enjoyable and meaningful things alone or with other people.

Relating to yourself in this positive way doesn't mean that you would instantaneously be freed from all loneliness and frustration. But it would mean that even if you felt low and unfulfilled, there would always be a part of you that loved and supported you. Because of this, it would be much easier for you to be on your own and to use this time to realise more of your potential.

If you feel inspired by the idea of becoming more of your own best friend, you can try the following exercise. You can also go back to page 108 and repeat the exercise that explains how to develop more love for yourself.

To Become Your Own Best Friend

- Take an empty exercise book and divide each page into two columns.

- In the left-hand column, write down moments and situations in which you have acted and spoken to yourself as if you are your best friend. For example, 'I encouraged myself to speak my mind in the meeting at work' or, 'I spoke lovingly to myself when I was lonely last night.'

- In the right-hand column, write down moments and situations in which you want to improve your way of relating to yourself. For example, 'I said a lot of nasty things to myself after I had eaten a whole bar of chocolate. Next time I will be friendlier to myself, even if I eat two bars. It's not the end of the world, after all.'

- If you keep writing in your diary, you will see that your ability to treat yourself in a friendlier way will increase tremendously.

Strengthening the contact with your Higher Consciousness

Another important way to get over painful feelings of loneliness is to strengthen your contact with your Higher

Consciousness. Actually, being lonely is *the* opportunity to find more access to the deepest source of love available in the universe. You don't have to be a religious person to feel this love; you just need to be open to the possibility of it. In the next exercise, you can explore the love that surrounds each one of us at all times and which, sadly, is often invisible.

To Experience the Love of Your Higher Consciousness

- Sit down quietly and relax as well as you can. If you like, you can put on a piece of lovely and relaxing music to support this process.

- Imagine that you are surrounded by a circle of beautiful divine beings who look at you with the deepest affection. Imagine that they wish you to be deeply happy and that you will find the love of your life.

- These loving beings can also see any faults or shortcomings you might have, but they don't judge you for them. Instead, they feel nothing but love and compassion for you, and wish from the bottom of their hearts that you might overcome any suffering or problem.

- Just sit silently and really feel this love. Open yourself up and really let it in; stay in this lovely feeling as long as you like. If negative thoughts or feelings threaten to overshadow your positive experience, just let them go and return to the positive images and feelings.

Remember that this exercise is not a fantasy. It is the truth as it has been taught by all spiritual teachers across the traditions and throughout the millennia. We *are* surrounded by loving and supportive beings who wish us nothing but love and pure bliss.

Not running away from yourself any more

Once you are equipped with the powerful tools of being your own best friend, as well as feeling the love of the divine and enlightened beings around you, you can tackle one of the most important steps to overcoming loneliness: stopping running away from yourself. For example, the next time you face some lonely, empty hours, don't try desperately to fill them up with numerous dates and activities. Instead, only plan to do things that really feel right to you and spend the rest of the time with yourself. Switch off the radio and television, and just sit down with a relaxing cup of tea and gently feel inside yourself. Be prepared to discover a whole range of emotions.

Your mood might swing from elation to depression within half an hour, or from loneliness to a beautiful feeling of spiritual connectedness. It is wise not to get hooked on any of these feelings, because you can't necessarily keep the good ones, nor can you get rid of all the difficult ones immediately. But you can observe everything that is going on inside you with a warm and loving attitude. As long as you can relate to yourself with this compassionate feeling, nothing really bad can happen to you no matter how bleak and horrible your life appears when you face your loneliness head-on.

At some point you might feel a desire to paint a picture or to write in your diary. These impulses are positive signs of your creativity emerging, and you should follow them up. As time goes by, you will discover that being alone is much easier when you stop running away from it and learn to relax into it. What seemed to be a horrible black hole at the beginning might emerge as some very interesting and meaningful time with yourself, which you can use for your creative hobbies and meditations.

Many people I have spoken to have gone through such a process. 'I would never have thought I could ever get over this terrible feeling of loneliness,' a woman told me just recently, 'but now I even value the time with myself. I don't even answer the telephone sometimes.'

I myself have felt very lonely in my life. But once I stopped running away from it, slowly, slowly my aversion to being alone transformed, and I learnt to use the time for going deeper into my creative self. I can honestly say that I have never felt more of the wonderful feeling of being close to my Higher Consciousness than in times of prolonged aloneness.

Strengthening your relationships with friends and family

The last tool for dealing with painful feelings of loneliness is strengthening and enjoying your relationships with your friends and family. Unfortunately, everyone in your family may not be your friend, and your best and true friends might not be related to you at all. A real friend is someone who really wants you to be happy, and who will support and help you in the process of becoming happy.

Finding new friends is probably easier than finding a soul-mate, but basically everything that is said in this book about finding a soulmate is just as true for finding really good friends. You need to wish for friends, develop as much love as possible in yourself and then go to places of mutual inter-est in order to meet potential friends. The process may take some time, but it will eventually bear fruit.

Equally, it is important to distance yourself from people who don't really care for you. Even if this will be hard at the beginning, it will be much more fruitful to spend time in your own loving company than with people who are repeat-edly critical or unsupportive of you. Of course, this doesn't mean that you should just give up on anyone who doesn't comply with all of your wishes. Particularly with family members, many of us have to learn the high art of diplomacy in order to share only those things that are enjoyable and to elegantly avoid topics of disagreement.

DEALING WITH REJECTION

The bad news is: rejections are even tougher than being lonely. The good news is: you only got rejected because there is somebody better for you. How is this possible?

If you have followed all the previous steps for finding a soulmate, you will have developed a lot of personal strength: you know what you want, you don't make bad compromises, you try to be kind and loving to yourself and others, and you have tackled your fears of being alone. In other words, you have become extraordinarily strong and loving, and you will therefore only match with someone who has similar positive qualities. And only two such extraordinary people are capable of being true soulmates.

When we look for a partner, many unconscious processes are going on that draw two people together or repulse them from each other. The more clearly we know what we want, the more powerfully these mechanisms will work. In other words, even if you are not conscious of it, the person who has rejected you might not fit your wish list exactly. No matter how strong the initial infatuation, on a deeper level this person will sense your strength. If they are not able to match it they may feel uncomfortable and withdraw. You can be glad of this, because you could never be happy with someone who hasn't got your power of mind and your integrity.

Rejections can be very painful, particularly if you really like someone. However, the more you have learnt to be your own best friend, the easier it will be to overcome those disappointments. Just repeat to yourself:

'This person might have some hidden disadvantages that I am not aware of. I only got this rejection because there is someone better waiting for me.'

Kate had been single for over a year when she met a man on a blind date she felt really excited about. He promised to phone, but when Kate didn't hear anything from him for over a week, her enthusiasm turned into a mixture of anger and depression. Finally, she phoned him herself and was told that he didn't have any further interest.

When Kate came to see me she cried and complained angrily about all the men who promise to phone but never do. I tried to explain to her that her own clarity has probably deterred someone who might not be in total alignment with her wishes. Kate listened to me but still felt upset. It was only when I reassured her that she had only had this rejection because there was someone better waiting for her that a smile crept onto her face. Intuitively, she sensed that I was right. She found a wonderful soulmate a few months later.

Chapter 10

Choosing the Right Partner

If there was only one rule that would determine whether your relationship would be happy it would be, 'Choose the right partner!' As most of us know, however, this rule is not very easy to follow. We can look at our comparison of how to grow flowers to learn more about how to achieve this high aim.

Once your seeds have grown into small seedlings, you need to choose the best and strongest plants and transfer them to bigger pots. This will give them more space and a better opportunity to unfold their potential. You also need to snip off the strongest middle shoot of each plant so that your seedlings will develop several side-shoots and grow into more bushy and satisfactory plants.

You need to go through a similar sorting out and snipping process when you are looking for a soulmate. Once you have met several people, you need to recognise and choose only the promising possibilities and 'snip off' the urge to unite sexually too early on. In this way, your relationship will develop much more richly and satisfactorily later on.

We need a good deal of time and all the clarity of our mind in the early days of a budding relationship in order to recognise whether it will have the potential to make us happy. As explained earlier, having sex can greatly inhibit our ability to see someone clearly. Even if we refrain from making love, most of us are not able to clearly recognise all the negative and positive dynamics, although the potential of the relationship is visible in the first two encounters.

It is therefore wise to invest more time and consideration into choosing our partner than we would into choosing a house, job and car together. Nothing will affect our well-being more strongly and profoundly than the quality of our love relationship.

Far too many people believe that they can instantly recognise their true soulmate, and fall in love on the basis of 'chemistry' and one or two half-digested ideas about what they want in life. Just recently, I talked to a woman who has a long line of dissatisfying relationship behind her. She had just met yet another new boyfriend and was very excited.

When I asked her how she knew that they were right for each other, she told me enthusiastically that they had the same taste in jewellery and films. I tell you, if it wasn't for the fact that I try to be a serene and empathetic person, I would have screamed in horror and pulled my hair in despair. Her superficial way of judging whether someone is right for her will lead to the break-up of her relationship just as likely as she will throw away a cheap prize she has won at a fun-fair.

In order to become able to distinguish a potential soulmate from just another better-than-nothing relationship, we have to use our feelings as well as our heads, and most of all we need to learn to recognise the warning signs.

FIND OUT MORE ABOUT YOUR POTENTIAL PARTNER

The most important thing is that you *feel* good with someone. However, having positive feelings alone is not enough to enable you to make the big decision as to whether someone is right for your. They could merely be a sign that you have a strong sexual chemistry, or that the person appears familiar to you.

If, therefore, you have a good feeling about a potential partner, you should start to ask them some questions. But one word of warning: don't take a catalogue of enquiries from your pocket and interrogate your candidate as if they were applying for a high-powered job. I have heard men who have spent time on the New York dating scene complaining about being treated like this. First and foremost it is important to feel at ease with each other. You therefore need to put your questions casually and light-heartedly into your conversations, and never let your potential partner feel that they are being scrutinised.

For example, when you ask your dating partner what he does for work or in his leisure time, listen first and foremost to what his answers tell you about his values and aims in life; don't ask him too directly about this. Or as you stroll together through the streets and you see some children, you can ask casually whether she likes children. If she says, 'Oh yes, a lot,' you can go one step further and ask her whether she wants some of her own. In this way you can gain important information about a person without making them feel that they are being checked out.

Making your dating partner comfortable is important because, as we have discussed before, your very first conversations will carry the information about the whole of your relationship. It is highly unlikely that a man will recognise a woman's beautiful feminine potential if she first gets on his nerves because of her aggressive interrogation. Although similar dynamics are often used in romantic films to enhance the tension (first they dislike each other, then they fall in love!), in the real world relationships work more according to the equation: as it begins, so it is likely to continue.

The following topics should all be clarified satisfactorily

before you go any further with your possible partner, no matter how much you desire her and no matter how charming he is.

Important topics to clarify

What are the professional and personal aims of your potential partner?

Try not to ask this question too directly because many people may not be able to answer it very clearly. Instead, try to read between the lines and make some conclusions. However, the compatibility of your aims and values in life is paramount, so you should try to find out as much as you can about these areas. If someone hasn't got any aims in life, this is important information, too.

What are the deepest values of your potential partner?

Again, don't ask this question too directly, because some people may be very perplexed by it. Instead, learn to get your information in a more indirect way. Maybe your dating partner will tell you about a conflict they had and how they resolved it. Then you can ask, 'Is it important to you to always make it up with people?' This will tell you something about how much they value peace and caring for others.

Another way to find out more about the values of your partner is to listen carefully to what they say about their previous relationships and why they didn't work out. Generally speaking, the deep values of a person show more clearly in the way they behave than in what they say; it is therefore wise to look carefully at how much someone's behaviour is driven by positive values like love.

On what terms is your potential partner with their previous partners?

Take your time to find this out. If people feel strong hurts, resentment, regrets or guilt towards their previous partners, they are not ready for a new relationship. It is also very revealing to listen to the problems your potential partner had in their previous relationships, as they are likely to repeat the part they played in them. Generally speaking, changing is not easy for people, and we only change when we put a lot of determination and effort into doing so.

What kind of commitment is your potential partner aiming for?

When you are on blind date you can ask at some point quite directly, 'So tell me, what kind of relationship are you aiming for in general?' But if you have met a person in different circumstances, you will have to be more careful. Maybe he will tell you that he is divorced and then you could say teasingly, 'And now you would never get married again!' Listen carefully, because if you want to get married and he is a marriage phobic, you had better look for someone else.

Does your potential partner want children?

There are an awful lot of break-ups of otherwise good relationships only because two partners failed to clarify this important topic in advance.

As a general rule, believe everything negative you hear. Now is *not* the time to look for the divine nature of a person and to try to think entirely positively while ignoring all the important warning signs. I can't count how often women have told me that they were in love with a 'wonderful' man, and that they couldn't believe it when this 'boyfriend' told them he 'only wanted fun'.

These women had usually mistaken his sexual passion as a sign that he wanted a committed relationship, even though he had clearly said the opposite. As a result, the women suffered deep agonies because in their hearts they were still lonely, although they were trying to maintain the illusion that they had found the man of their dreams.

Generally speaking, if a woman tells you that she still hates her former husband, count your losses and move on. Equally, if a man tells you that a feeling of love is just the result of chemistry in your brain, bring your meeting to a rapid end and comfort yourself with a late-night film. In both cases, you will gain nothing by trying to convince yourself that this person has otherwise positive features. It just wouldn't work.

You will also have to treat everything positive you hear with great caution – check whether what your potential partner says and what they do is in harmony. Finding this out will take time and clarity of mind, so I strongly suggest again that you don't rush into choosing a partner. The six relationship test questions in the next section explain how you can evaluate further whether someone is really right for you.

THE SIX RELATIONSHIP TEST QUESTIONS

It can be hard to be clear and discerning when you meet a potential partner and all the suppressed neediness of your time alone raises its head and demands instant gratification. The six relationship test questions can effectively help you to find out whether someone really suits you. Moreover, by answering these questions you will even be able to predict the future to a certain degree, because they can reveal most of the important dynamics of a relationship even if you have met someone only two or three times.

Before you try out these questions on a potential partner, I suggest that you first use them on one of your previous partners, imagining it is the evening after your second meeting. If you find that by answering the questions you could have found out more or less everything that was to follow, you can trust the results of these questions more when you use them with new potential partners.

The questions

1. How did I feel in myself and about myself when I was with my potential partner?

2. What kind of view does my potential partner have about the world, and do I want to share it?

3. Did I notice any warning signs or character flaws in my potential partner?

4. Are our most important aims and values in life compatible?

5. For men: did she appreciate what I did for her? For women: did I like what he did for me?

6. Do I fancy my potential partner?

The responses

1. How did I feel in myself and about myself when I was with my potential partner?

When trying to decide whether a potential partner is right for them, many people attempt to make up their minds by evaluating the character and looks of the person. However, when you work with the first of the six relationship questions, you do the opposite. Instead of asking how you felt *about your potential partner*, you turn inside and ask yourself, 'How did I feel *in myself* and *about myself*?' This indirect approach will give you much more important information than if you were merely looking at the other person.

Many people have noticed that they feel differently in themselves and about themselves when they are with different people, irrespective of how they felt before their meeting. In the presence of one person they may feel confident, talented and beautiful, while with another they might feel inexplicably tired, nervous or even unattractive. These feelings are no accident – they are important data that you can use to find out whether someone is the right partner for you.

You don't need to be able to interpret your feelings, and it doesn't matter whether they are caused by your own 'neurotic material' or by the other person. At the end of the day, they boil down to the same fact – that this person is not right for you at this moment. No matter how pretty and inspiring you find a woman, if you continue to feel like a loser in her presence she will not be the right person for you. Conversely, if you feel more contented and special when you are with a potential partner than you did before, you will know that you are on a very good track.

In order to answer this first question correctly, you have to be very honest and put to one side the strong desire you might feel to find a partner. In particular, you have to look out for whether you felt more tense or more relaxed in the presence of the other person, whether you felt more or less confident, and whether you felt stronger or weaker. It can also be interesting to check whether you felt more or less attractive and beautiful.

All these feelings are caused by an intricate feedback system that takes place on a more or less unconscious level when two people meet. There is no point in blaming the other person if you felt negative; this is just a sign that you might not suit each other completely. You should also by no means give up on someone you really like only because you felt challenged in your confidence in their presence. On a blind date, for example, it is normal to feel nervous or even a bit anxious.

The six relationship test questions can only give you a broad guideline as to whether someone suits you, and as I have said many times before, you need to give yourself plenty of time to check someone out.

2. What kind of view does my potential partner have about the world, and do I want to share it?

In order to answer this question, you can do an interesting little exercise that can tell you a lot about your potential partner and will also help you to develop your empathetic abilities.

For a moment, imagine you *are* your potential partner. Sit like they would sit, imagine wearing their clothes, and look around the room and out of the window 'through their eyes'. Without trying too hard, just watch what comes spontaneously to your mind about what kind of place the world is for your potential partner. Do you see problems and struggles through their eyes, or fun and adventure? Do you see some hardship and pessimism, or meaning and love?

Once you have received a clue about the kind of world your potential partner lives in, ask yourself whether you would like to share their world. With the passage of time, no one can avoid taking on parts of their partner's character and part of the way they perceive the world. This is due to the unavoidable merging process we talked about earlier.

Sometimes people marry someone with many problems in order to help them to look at the world with happier eyes. These people are idealistic, and they are convinced that they can help their partner through their love and their care. However, instead of drawing their partner into their happier and idealistic world, the opposite usually happens. The 'helping' partner is drawn down into the misery of their unhappy partner, because the person with the heavier and more negative feelings dominates the overall emotional atmosphere of the relationship. This sad dynamic has been demonstrated in millions of codependant relationships that are so debilitating that the 'helping' partner often finds it almost impossible to get out of them.

A person can only be a real soulmate for you if the way they see the world makes you feel excited and joyful, and if it harmonises with your deepest values.

3. Did I notice any warning signs or character flaws in my potential partner?

If a person displays any character flaws in the very first few meetings with a new partner, this is a great warning sign. People usually try to show their best side when they are with a potential partner for the first time. If they are unable to conceal their more negative side even then, there is little hope that they will do so in the future. Remember, as a relationship begins, so it is likely to continue.

Even if the negative behaviour of a potential partner is not directed at you but at other people, it should set off loud alarm bells in your head. Unfortunately, we all show our worst side to no one more than to our intimate partner. We may never scream in frustration at our annoying boss, but may well do so at our beloved partner at some point.

This dynamic is due to the fact that we are less controlled with people we love. Therefore, if someone talks in a scathing and degrading way about other people, it will only be a matter of time before they do the same to you once the honeymoon enthusiasm has worn off a little. Here is a list of warning signs and character flaws that you should look out for.

• **Not keeping one's word** It might seem like a little thing that someone doesn't phone when they have said they would, but the ability to keep one's word is essential in a soulmate relationship. In fact, a good marriage contains a range of hundreds of agreements, from how to put the cutlery in the drawer, to the key promise of not sleeping with other people. If someone repeatedly breaks any of these agreements, the relationship will become very frustrating. Therefore, if you already notice broken promises (even small ones) in the first few meetings, this is not a good sign.

• **Lying** If someone lies to you it will undermine any trust you may have in them. Even if you find it understandable or even endearing that someone tries to make themselves more 'interesting, younger or richer' in order to attract you, this is not a good basis from which to start a soulmate relationship. Trust is one of the most important foundations on which two people can grow in love, and if this basis has already been weakened in the very first meetings it will be difficult to repair it later on.

- **Treating you or others in an uncaring way** Don't ignore little signs of selfish behaviour, whether they are directed at you or at others. They are only likely to grow and be directed at you once your partner is more familiar and relaxed with you. It is also a warning sign if your potential partner has treated their previous partners in an uncaring way, because they are likely to repeat this behaviour with you. People don't change easily, and it is a mistake to think that someone will be much more caring with you if they have been unloving towards previous partners.

- **Aggressive language** Some people use swear words, and there is nothing wrong with this if you don't mind it. But if a potential partner speaks with real aggression this is a warning sign, because at some point this anger will be directed at you. You had better bow out while you are still not involved. Equally, if someone has a history of losing their temper, it is a big risk to start a relationship with them. Most people don't change a lot as they get older and just continue behaving in the way they have always done.

- **Strong black and white attitudes** Some people have extreme opinions ('people who eat meat are bad' or 'people who have sex before marriage are sinners'), and you are likely to get into trouble once they direct such opinions at you. It is a sign of maturity to see the many shades of grey that exist in every being, and to abstain from condemning one person while glorifying another.

- **Overspending or meanness** If someone displays traits of meanness even during your first meeting, you can just imagine how mean they will be later on when they are more relaxed with you. It is best to make a big bow around such people. A person who overspends is no better – you can only have a good relationship with a person who is mature enough to deal with their money in a responsible way.

- **Putting themselves down excessively or boasting** Genuine humility is a beautiful character trait. If, however, someone has very little self-confidence this is a warning sign, because you can only be loved by someone who can love themselves. On the other hand, if the pendulum swings in the other direction and someone talks about their successes in a way that is too conceited, you had better distance yourself from this person as well.

- **History of being unfaithful** If someone has repeatedly betrayed their former partners, this is a major warning sign. There is no reason to believe that this person will stay loyal to you if they haven't put a great deal of effort into changing themselves.

- **Substance abuse** Much has been said and written about codependent relationships, but it is still not easy to recognise the early-warning signs of a budding or even full-grown alcoholic or drugs abuser. The amount of alcohol drinking that you will find acceptable in your potential partner will strongly depend on how much you like to drink yourself, but generally speaking drugs or a great deal of alcohol cannot co-exist with a real soulmate relationship.

- **Addictive behaviour** Addictive behaviour like working or eating too much are other warning signs that shouldn't be overlooked. Also be on your guard if someone tells you that they had an addiction earlier on in their life that hasn't been treated with a therapy or in a self-help group.

It is very difficult to stop an addiction all by oneself, and there is a danger that this negative form of behaviour will go on and disrupt the happiness in your relationship.

- **Violence with former partners** If someone tells you that they have been violent with a former partner, cut the meeting short and say good-bye as quickly as possible. Letting a potentially violent person into your life is just not worth the risk.

4. Are our most important aims and values in life compatible?

In order to answer this question you obviously need to know clearly what your own values in life are. The most important aim for a true soulmate relationship is the wish to love and grow in love with your partner. This is the only value that can bring deep and lasting happiness to romantic relationships. No amount of sexual passion, exhilarating fun and mutual interests of any kind can bring you the deep satisfaction that can arise from feeling loved and loving someone, and from the wish to get over any obstacle that might obstruct this positive attitude.

The following list can give you some clues to finding out whether someone's commitment to love is more than just lip-service. Your potential partner:

- *Continuously* treats you lovingly and generously in every respect.

- Is sympathetic about your weaknesses and ready to comply with most of your needs.

- And you are able to quickly resolve little misunderstandings.

- Speaks with respect and care about their previous partners and doesn't harbour major resentments against them any more.

- Didn't inflict any unnecessary pain on their previous partner either during their relationship or during their split-up.

- Fulfils all their responsibilities to their own children with dedication and love.

- Tries to overcome problems with their own family and to develop positive relationships with everyone in it.

- Treats other people with respect and care.

- Doesn't harbour major resentment or hatred against anything or anyone in the world.

- Is not obsessed with anything so much that it would decrease their ability to love you.

- Tells you explicitly that they want to grow in love.

- Follows a path of personal or spiritual development that increases their ability to love (for example a path of self-development, prayer, meditation or healing).

Don't assume that you know everything about someone's values once you know what religion they belong to. 'Being' a Christian, for example, is by no means a guarantee that someone really lives according to the Christian values of love and forgiveness. You have to be very clear and discerning to find out what someone believes in *deep down* by seeing how they behave in many different situations. Being on the same spiritual path is by no means a guarantee that you will find happiness together. It is much more important for two people to *genuinely* want to grow in love than for them to go to the same church.

Besides the all-important value of love, you obviously need to clarify whether your other important aims in life are compatible. The most important of these are whether you both want the same sort of commitment, and whether you both want children. If you fancy someone who is on the same wave-length in all of these three areas – love, commitment and children – you will find that you will both be able to happily tolerate many otherwise different interests and character traits in each other.

5. For men: did she appreciate what I did for her? For women: did I like what he did for me?

For some people, these questions might appear terribly sexist, as they place women into a 'pathetic' receiving role and put a large burden on men to always be strong care-givers, even if they don't feel like this. I can understand their rebellion, because for many years I thought along the same lines. But once I saw clearly that no deep romantic fulfilment can be achieved if you have these attitudes, I threw them overboard once and for all.

As long as a man has a masculine sexual orientation, he will gain most romantic and erotic fulfilment from being in the leading and giving role. He will not be able to feel fully confident and strong as long as he looks to his woman to be the same as him in *every* way, or even to take the lead. On the other hand, as long as a woman has a feminine sexual orientation, she will experience most romantic and erotic fulfilment if she feels cared for and supported. This doesn't mean that she couldn't care for herself, but it will provide her with a possibility of finding much deeper fulfilment than she could find on her own.

So, if you are a man, try to initiate things in order to please your partner, but check to see that your efforts are appreciated. Only if you feel comfortable and confident in your masculine side will you be able to find lasting romance with this woman. All this obviously doesn't mean that you can never lean back and be in the receiving role – however, if your feminine receptive side takes over completely, the delightful dance of romance will stop.

If you are a woman, see if what he does voluntarily for you

makes you feel good and supported. This certainly doesn't mean that you are condemned to exist in a totally passive role. You can always make suggestions and give hints about what you like. If, however, your masculine side takes over and you initiate and control most of what is happening, you will soon find that there is not a trace of romance left between you and your partner.

6. Did I fancy my potential partner?

Sometimes people meet someone who fulfils every single relationship test question to the letter, but they can't imagine having sex with this person because they are just not their type. That is really bad luck. For many people, however, erotic attraction grows over time, and it is a promising sign if they at least don't feel sexually repulsed by their potential partner.

Unfortunately, this last relationship test question is used by many people as the *only* means of determining whether they want to start a relationship with someone. It's therefore no surprise that they find out later that their values and aims in life are incompatible, and will make deep and blissful intimacy impossible.

There you are. These are the six relationship test questions, and they can show you quite reliably whether you have a chance of finding true and *lasting* happiness with someone. If you really like and fancy a person, you should ask yourself these questions several times and deliberately focus more on the negative aspects. It is actually not a good time to practise too much positive thinking while you are choosing a life partner!

If any of these relationship test questions is answered in a unsatisfactory way, this is a strong sign that you haven't found your soulmate yet. These six questions have been tried and tested in many relationships, and have proven over and over again that they can predict with a very high likelihood how a relationship will develop. A client of mine,

Barbara, answered them remembering her second meeting with Thomas.

1. How did I feel in myself and about myself when I was with Thomas?
Confident. I felt I could explain to him my deep spiritual values and I enjoyed being able to influence him.

2. What kind of view did Thomas have about the world and did I want to share it?
For Thomas, the world was quite a depressing and lonely place. I didn't want to share this world, but I wanted to show him that there is much more joy possible.

3. Did I notice any warning signs or character flaws in Thomas?
He was not very punctual.

4. Were our most important aims and values in life compatible?
I think we had similar spiritual goals.

5. Did I like what Thomas did for me?
He didn't do anything remarkable for me at that point.

6. Did I fancy Thomas?
A great deal.

Barbara went on to marry Thomas. They had a fantastic sex-life, two children and numerous conflicts about their spiritual aims, which led to their divorce sixteen years later. Barbara had felt continuously pulled down by Thomas's 'negative outlook on life', and she was deeply sad that she hadn't been able to share any of her joy and meaning in life with her husband.

You see, it was already all there, the second time they met! Superficially, they had similar spiritual aims, and they had a great erotic wave-length, which was enough to convince

them that they were meant for each other. But on a deeper
level they didn't suit each other because their outlook on life
was incompatible. At the beginning of their relationship,
they had an even deal between them that helped them to get
over this incompatibility. They had unconsciously agreed
that Barbara would teach Thomas the deep spiritual joys she
could feel, and that he was a kind of student of hers who
would give her lots of appreciation back. During this time,
they had quite happily lived a kind of hippy life on a
minimum amount of money.

Once the children arrived, Thomas was thrown into the
role of the breadwinner, which put enormous pressure on
him, and he didn't want to be Barbara's 'student' any more.
That meant their even deal was broken, and from that point
onwards their relationship went downhill. As I have
explained before, it is the partner who is more miserable
who will dominate the atmosphere of the whole relationship.
This happened in Barbara and Thomas's case, and it led to
the complete break-up of their relationship a few years later.

As you see, it is not enough to have a positive result in only
some of these test questions. If you want to have a real soulmate relationship, all six questions need to be answered
positively. The following test questions were answered by
Robert, who has a truly wonderful relationship with his wife
Anna. As in the previous example, Robert tried to recall how
he felt on his second meeting, when he first got to know his
future wife.

1. How did I feel in myself and about myself when I was
with Anna?
*I felt quite confident, happy and also interesting because she listened
to what I had to say.*

2. What kind of view did Anna have about the world and
did I want to share it?
I got the impression that she thought it was a fun place with some

magic in it and that is was important to follow one's spiritual path. I definitely wanted to share her world.

3. Did I notice any warning signs or character flaws in Anna?
No.

4. Were our most important aims and values in life compatible?
I wasn't quite sure at that point, but mostly yes.

5. Did Anna appreciate what I did for her?
She seemed glad to come on the walk I suggested.

6. Did I fancy Anna?
Yes, definitely.

TAKE YOUR TIME BEFORE YOU COMMIT

Don't think that all true soulmate relationships 'must' start with a feeling of love at first sight, and that instant recognition is the only way to get to know each other. This is by no means the case, and no matter what romantic novels say, love at first sight is no guarantee that only exhilarating happiness will follow. In the worst scenarios it could merely be a sign of strong sexual chemistry, or that someone could evoke some very strong feelings in you. In fact, many relationships that have started with this instant infatuation have ended in total disaster when it has dawned on one or both partners that they have got it completely wrong.

Real soulmate relationship can start in many ways – slowly and quietly, through many detours and misunderstandings, or with a big bang. You might even feel nothing whatsoever when you and your soulmate-to-be meet the very first time, and your love for each other may only grow over time. Whether your relationship starts slowly or quickly, one day you will find yourself thinking, 'This person might be my soulmate.' At this point, you can use the six relationship test questions to find out whether you are roughly on the right track. But you must be careful even if all these questions have been answered to your total satisfaction, because in this phase of your budding relationship there are four pitfalls you have to avoid.

The four pitfalls

1. Having sex with each other before you have made a basic commitment.

2. Having sex with others.

3. Ignoring the law of an even deal.

4. Making a premature commitment.

1. Having sex with your potential soulmate before you have made a basic commitment

Don't get me wrong, I am not an enemy of sexual liberation. On the contrary, I think it is wonderful that in our society we are free to explore our sexuality unhampered by the force of having to marry for life. If, however, the time comes when you *want* to marry, sexuality should be treated as something extremely precious. You should only share it when all the conditions are right and when you and your partner have promised whole-heartedly to love each other in a monogamous relationship.

Coming to this point will take some time and during these weeks or months it would be a big mistake to unite sexually with your potential soulmate. Why is this so?

First of all, as I have explained before, having sex will blind you to seeing your potential partner clearly. The unavoidable merging process between two lovers takes place most strongly through the exchange of sexual energy and fluids. Once that has happened, you can't see your partner entirely from 'your point of view' any more. In other words, your ability to judge whether someone is right for you will be drastically reduced after you have had sex with them. This is particularly true for women, who tend to be more emotionally engaged in the sexual act then men. Have you have ever wondered why people fall in love with someone who is so obviously unsuitable for them? One of the answers is that they had sex too early, and committed to their partner merely on the basis of sexual infatuation.

Although the whole dynamic of a relationship *can* be seen in the first one or two encounters between two people, this doesn't mean that everyone *is able* to see all the potential problems that they will encounter with their partner. Even if you use the six relationship test questions, it can be terribly tempting to lie to yourself when you strongly desire someone. In other words, keeping your eyes open and being realistic about your potential partner is difficult enough. But when you have sex with the person it will be nearly impossible and it might take months, if not years, before you finally wake up to the truth.

There are other reasons to stay celibate in the early stages of a new relationship. As we have already discussed, men find it harder than women to make strong commitments, because unrepressed masculine energy has a tendency to strive for power and freedom. Therefore many men will only want to give up their beloved freedom when they are *very* sure that they have found the right woman. But if they can have sex and closeness with someone without having to promise anything, some men will find it even harder to fulfil their inner need for commitment.

On an energy level, refraining from making love means that the sexual energy that is aroused in the first attraction between two people can go up and reach their hearts, where is can be transformed into love and the wish to commit. But for some people opening their heart doesn't come easy, and they have to feel a very strong desire before they can allow themselves to be touched in this deep and vulnerable spot.

So if their desire for each other is satisfied in a sexual union too early, it dissipates and cannot be built up to the necessary amount in order to help someone feel their deep wish to love and to commit whole-heartedly.

As you can see, it is often the woman who can loose more if she has sex too early with her potential partner, and therefore it is in her own interest to withhold her sexuality until she and her soulmate have found in their hearts the love and the wish to commit to each other, which is the only thing that can satisfy them in the long run.

This withholding has nothing to do with playing 'hard to get' in order to manipulate a man into a commitment he would not otherwise have made. It is simply in the deepest interest of anyone who wants a true soulmate relationship to delay making love. A mature and loving man will understand and value this process.

To put it a bit more drastically: no matter how sexually liberated a woman is, if she wants to have a committed relationship she should under *no circumstances* initiate making love for the first time. There are two reasons for this. Firstly, it is not very romantic and secondly, it will make an undecided man more uncertain whether to pursue the relationship, or even push him away completely.

2. Having sex with others

Having sex with other people while you are dating someone with whom you might want to start a serious relationship is even worse than having sex with your potential soulmate. Strictly speaking, you are already betraying the one you are pretending to love. The deep love and commitment that makes a true soulmate relationship can only thrive on the condition that two partners completely reserve their sexual energies for each other, whether in the early stages of the relationship or later on. Only then can the wonderful merging process between two people take place, enriching them both in the most wonderful way possible.

I once spoke to a man, James, who started a relationship with a young woman who needed a lot of time before she was ready to make love. James agreed to her needs superficially, but had sex the whole time with an old lover of his in order to satisfy his sexual needs. Not surprisingly, he never came to the point where he could whole-heartedly commit to his young girlfriend, although they dated each other for over three years. Eventually, she had enough of his lukewarm attitude and found herself another boyfriend. That was the moment when James's energy finally reached his heart, and he suddenly noticed how much he wanted to be with her. But it was too late, and as a consequence he suffered a great deal.

3. Ignoring the law of an even deal
At no time can you afford to ignore the law of an even deal, because it is at the core of what will bring you lasting happiness and satisfaction in every relationship. But it is *particularly* important to be strict about applying this rule in the early stages of a relationship, as they will determine how the rest of the relationship will develop.

Too many women make the mistake of pursuing a man too aggressively, and don't have the patience to wait and see what will come from him voluntarily. In the worst cases, a woman may even start to give a man money, which is like committing 'relationship suicide'. One day, she will realise that she has been betrayed, or she will wake up beside a man who is inexplicably angry at her (because he just doesn't want to be 'in her debt' any more).

On the other hand, men cannot afford to be lazy and undetermined at this early stage, as their attitude will hurt their girlfriend. Her disappointment will make it hard for her to give him her surrender.

If your choice of partner has been wise, this early commitment to behave according to the law of an even deal will bring you satisfaction for the moment as well as later on. If, however, you are with someone who isn't right for you, your firm application of the law of an even deal will quickly bring out the incompatibility between you two.

If you are a man and you are pursuing a woman whole-heartedly only to find that her reaction is lukewarm, you will be better off finding someone who will appreciate your efforts more. Equally, if you are a woman and you feel you can only have a relationship with a man when all the initiative comes from your side, you should not try to put up with this situation. Instead, try to wait and see what comes from his side. If it is little or nothing, you will be better off moving on. Although the break-up will hurt, it is best to split up now than to have to go through a major break-up later on.

4. Making a premature commitment

If you really like and fancy someone, it would be wise to have a look at your initial wish list and to really talk to each other about what it would be like to be a couple. Leisurely and playfully compare all your attitudes, whether they have to do with personal growth, having fun or who should be respons-ible for earning the money and doing the housework. Include talking about your deepest values and what they really mean in terms of everyday behaviour, and how you plan to get over your future conflicts and disagreements. Would your relationship be precious enough to include going to a relationship counsellor if you got stuck in a problem?

It might feel scary to probe all these topics so early on, but no matter what your potential partner says you can only win. If you are on the same wave-length you can rejoice, and if you aren't you can move on before it is too late.

Talking to each other is not enough. You also have to check whether the behaviour of your potential partner is in alignment with what they say. As a colleague of mine puts it, 'Watch out for whether the video matches the audio.' If a woman tells you how committed she is to grow in love but tries to control and improve you already at this point, you should be very suspicious. Equally, if a man tells you how much he wants a committed relationship but stands you up repeatedly, you should consider this to be a real warning sign. Also, if your partner is inspiring and charming to *you* but has numerous conflicts with other people, you should know by now that it will only be a matter of time before these conflicts will surface in your relationship as well.

Generally speaking, in this early phase women should ensure that they are happy with what a man does for them voluntarily, and how he responds to their *gentle* suggestions.

This is not the time to have arguments about him being more considerate, or to improve any of his behaviour. Instead, make sure you are happy with your potential partner just the way he is.

Men, on the other hand, should focus on how to care for their woman, and ensure that they succeed in this.

You can always ask your girlfriend what she likes, but if nothing that you do is ever good enough and she is never really happy with you, you will almost certainly encounter a lot of problems in the future.

This phase of checking each other out is a phase of uncertainty, and that can be hard to bear if every cell in you screams for the safety of the loving embrace of your soulmate. But remember, none of your previous relationships would have failed if you had been a bit wiser in the beginning, and if you had made a choice that had taken into account your deeper needs. Now you have the chance to be more clever. I can only urge you to use it and to not succumb to sexual infatuation, family traps and unresolved issues from your past.

Even if you have the most 'amazing astrological aspects', or find each other in the 'most unbelievable coincidences', this is by no means a guarantee that you are meant for each other. I once spoke to a woman, Ruth, who told me how she got to know her partner. He had phoned her for the first time on the birthday of her daughter, and the date of his birthday fell on the date of the birthday of her son. She continued to relate to me how many more important dates in their lives coincided, and how she had taken all this as a sign from God that she should marry this man. Not surprisingly, her relationship is not an easy one.

Another woman I know always asks her spiritual teachers to check through divination whether her new relationships have potential. She always receives a 'yes', but contrary to these positive omens none of her relationships has ever worked out. However, despite all her heartache she still hasn't learnt the lesson that only she herself can truly know what is good for her, and that she is fully responsible for her decisions.

Grasping at the most ludicrous facts, like these women do, in order to believe that one has found one's soulmate is just another proof of how people can be blinded by their desire. I therefore suggest again: *only* when you have clarified *all* your concerns, and when *all* the six relationship questions have been answered positively over a period of at least twenty meetings, can you move forwards to make a commitment to each other and start a serious relationship.

HOW TO MAKE A COMMITMENT TO EACH OTHER

Some people try to start a relationship by going to bed with each other, and if that feels good they assume they have a committed relationship. This is a big mistake. It can lead to

a lot of heartache, because people have all sorts of ideas
about what making love stands for, and by no means everyone takes it as a sign that they will have a committed
relationship.

A commitment to have a soulmate relationship should be
made with *words*, and both people should know each other
well enough to be able trust their partner. Having sex
should only happen *after* two people have said that they love
each other, and that they want a committed and monogamous relationship. By this time it should also be clear how
you two want to take care of contraception and the prevention of sexually transmitted diseases. Only in these
circumstances can having sex be elevated to its most worthy
position, and become making love.

As we have discussed, it is often the woman who desires a
commitment most strongly, in particular if a couple has a
strong polarity of masculine and feminine energy. Feminine
energy strives more strongly for closeness and security,
while masculine energy wants to expand and be free. This
situation is a delicate issue, and should be approached
in a skilful way. A woman will have won nothing if she asks a
man too directly to make a commitment, because she
might get an answer that is just lip-service formulated to
please her.

It is therefore advisable for a woman to talk and behave in
an inviting way, but to withhold herself sexually in order to
encourage the man's desire to come closer to her and
commit. For example, if he wants to initiate sex, she could
kiss him but then say, 'I'm not sure I am ready for more. I
only want to make love with someone with whom I am in a
serious relationship,' and leave it totally up to him to
respond to this. This has nothing to do with being manipu-
lative, but is the most prudent behaviour possible in these
circumstances.

Generally speaking, most men and women will know relatively soon whether they want a serious relationship with

someone or not. If a person can't make up their mind for months on end, the problem lies most likely within themselves. In that case it is appropriate to address the issue directly and to ask your potential partner what they want. If they still don't know, it is probably best to look for someone else. Remember, as a relationship starts, so it is likely to continue.

Part III

Keeping a Soulmate

Chapter 11

The Stages of Romantic Relationships

If you have found a relationship according to the guidelines in this book you are very lucky, because you will have little to fear in terms of future problems and heartaches. Choosing the right partner is really the most difficult step, and once you have mastered this everything will be quite easy from then on. A relationship with the 'right' partner would look like this:

- You are both dedicated to growing in love, and you both follow a path of personal development that will help you to overcome any obstacle that might be in the way of this high aim.

- You both genuinely care for each other as much as you care for yourselves, and both of you also have a loving and caring attitude towards all other beings.

- Your personal and professional aims in life are compatible, which means that neither of you has to make major sacrifices in terms of lifestyle or values in order to be together.

- You both feel loved and cared for by each other.

- You both feel happy, confident and inspired in each other's presence.

- You are erotically attracted to each other.

- You both have integrity, and you can fully rely on each other's word.

- You have not noticed and ignored any character flaws and warning signs.

If you and your partner have such a relationship, you can lean back and smile broadly. If, however, your partnership only partly equals the description above, there is no need to despair. By applying the guidelines in Part III, many relationships can be transformed and become much more satisfying.

In order for this to happen, both you and your partner need to be willing to make the necessary changes. I won't lie to you; if your partner doesn't want to change there is not much you can do. Unfortunately, the clever manipulation technique that will make your spouse willingly comply with any of your wishes still waits to be invented.

Every romantic relationship typically goes through three stages, which are honeymoon, struggle and maturity. The length of these stages can vary between weeks and years, and depends largely on the maturity of both partners and their ability to get over the struggle stage as quickly as possible. While ordinary relationships seldom develop past the struggle stage, people in soulmate relationships typically spend very little time in it; if they are lucky they can move more or less straight from the honeymoon phase to the maturity stage, which feels like being 'in love forever'.

THE HONEYMOON STAGE

People's opinions about the honeymoon are greatly divided. For some it is a paradise on Earth, while for others it is clearly a time of insanity. There have even been serious scientific studies on how the thinking and feeling patterns of people 'in love' are very similar to those of people with compulsive disorders. The researchers measured how often people thought 'compulsively' about their new partner, and how their pulse and heart rate dramatically increased when they came into contact with their new love. They concluded that these patterns were clearly just as 'ill' as those of people with severe neurotic disorders.

I believe that once you have made a *wise* choice, being in love is the most wonderful madness you can experience. The fantastic state of euphoria, the unbelievable sexual passion and the blinding love are better than anything that Mother Earth can offer her children. There is no need to hold yourself back, and you can fully enjoy what you have prepared and worked for so hard. The honeymoon is harvest time, and you can allow yourself to dive deeply into this fantastic experience without any fear of regretting it afterwards.

The law of an even deal in the honeymoon stage
Usually the types of problem that result from ignoring the law of an even deal are no great risk at this point, because both partners are at their best. If the woman utters only the slightest wish, the man will jump up and serve her with everything her heart desires. And she will pay him back with a willing surrender of her heart and her body. In other words: it's a paradise.

It is, however, still wise to keep the law of an even deal at the back of your mind in order to avoid any gross violation. Even if you want to give your partner *everything*, hold back if you notice that your generosity is not met with equal measure. This has nothing to do with being mean, but a lot to do with being wise. If you give too much, your partner may not appreciate your effort, because they could experience your giving as a mounting debt which they must give back equally, and they may not be ready for that.

If you want the giving and taking in your relationship to increase, go slowly, and give only *a little* more than your partner has given you, then wait for what will come back. If this is not satisfying you can *gently* ask for more, and you will often find that your partner will be only too happy to comply.

Additionally, don't swallow any frustration, but be brave and discuss any hurt that your partner inflicts on you. If you are too forgiving, your inner hurt will only cause you to slowly but surely become more distant and resentful. Whatever conflict you can resolve successfully at this stage will serve you as a good foundation once you enter the struggle stage and have to solve a multitude of quarrels.

The commitment to love each other and to grow in love in the honeymoon stage

There is probably no other time in a couple's relationship when their commitment to love each other is stronger than in the honeymoon stage. At this point, we usually think that our partner is the most amazing and wonderful person in the whole universe, and our love for each other comes effortlessly and is not challenged in any way. Under these circumstances, even the most difficult person will soften and become a messenger of peace.

At this point in a relationship, it is most important to pay close attention to the proper build-up of commitment and to avoid hastening things. Some people feel the urge to move in with each other as soon as they enter the honeymoon stage. However, for men and women whose long-term goal is to get married, this is not a good idea. On a practical level, living together and being married can feel very similar, and the partner who is more afraid of making a commitment will have little or no incentive to make this final move if they can 'have it all' without giving a deeper promise. However, being married is much more than living together and sharing the everyday household chores. Our deep commitments have a great influence on our entire outlook on life, and will determine how much meaning and fulfilment we can find. In other words, the more someone can happily and whole-heartedly commit, be it to other people, to a vocation or to a spiritual path, the more fulfilment they will find in life. But many people need time to understand this truth, and a commitment that is imposed is worse than making no commitment at all.

Therefore if your goal is to get married, you should only move in with each other once you and your partner know that you want to make this final commitment. In this way, living together will be your engagement time and will lead to marriage rather than to nothing.

Once again, it is mostly harder for the man than the woman to find the courage to make a whole-hearted commitment. For the sake of both romance and honesty, it is best if the man makes a beautiful 'old-fashioned' proposal. A woman can give hints, but she should painstakingly avoid making a proposal herself because this lack of romance will be felt during the rest of the marriage. If, however, you have followed the advice in this book, you should have clarified long ago how much your partner wants to get married in general. The build-up of commitment should therefore be a matter of timing, and you shouldn't experience a nasty surprise when it turns out that your partner 'only wants to have fun'.

If you are a woman and feel that despite your hints, and despite what your boyfriend has said earlier, he is dragging his feet in terms of proposing, at some point you can say something like this, 'I really want to get married. It is one of my most important goals in life, and a relationship that doesn't lead to marriage isn't worth pursuing for ever.'

Then leave it totally up to him to respond. If you still haven't received a proposal within a month, you might want to consider moving on.

The male–female polarity in the honeymoon stage

There is no other time in romantic relationships when male and female energies are more polarised than during the honeymoon stage. This means that women are never more in their feminine side and men are never more in their masculine side than when they have just fallen in love.

It is exactly these dynamics that make for the euphoria and bliss that we can experience when we are attracted and finally unite with someone who is so wonderfully different from ourselves. The masculine urge to possess and conquer is met by sweet, feminine surrender, which makes the emotional and sexual union ever so delightful and passionate.

There is probably no other time when even an 'alternative' man and an otherwise 'feminist' woman might enjoy old-fashioned rituals like the man opening the car door for the woman or helping her into her coat. Only at these times, when people can allow themselves to relish their gender identity, can they come to understand that these rituals have nothing to do with oppressing the woman. On the contrary, they bring out her tenderest and most vulnerable aspects so that she can enjoy the strength and care of a loving man even more deeply.

Going more deeply into your gender identity can make people feel vulnerable, because it can make men a bit inse-cure in their new strength, and women feel soft and defenceless. But it is exactly the process of allowing yourself to be so vulnerable that makes this dynamic so delightful. It is letting go of our usual mechanisms of control and defence that makes the honeymoon into a paradise on Earth.

The unavoidable merging process between two partners in the honeymoon stage

The honeymoon stage is the time when the merging process between two people takes place in the most dramatic way. Hours of loving conversation and eye contact over candle-lit dinners, romantic strolls under moonlight with tender kisses, and passionate nights afterwards serve only one aim: uniting with our partner in as many ways as possible.

The greater the difference between the characters of two lovers, and the stronger their male–female polarity, the stronger will be the magnetism that draws them together again and again in a romantic and sexual embrace.

If we were clairvoyant we could witness how two people in love literally take on the energies of their partner and slowly fill in their own deficiencies and weaknesses. For example, it is a typical dynamic that a person with a hard and neglectful childhood feels drawn to someone who had a lot of support as a child and vice versa.

The person with the difficult childhood is often strong and achieving, but misses warmth and unconditional love. Therefore they feel drawn to someone who can provide this. On the other hand, people who felt loved and even spoilt as children tend to lack discipline and stamina, and often feel attracted to someone who displays just these character traits. In such a couple, one person gives the other what they are missing, and they both have the opportunity to slowly take on the character traits of their partner and finally find in themselves what they have missed all their lives.

Other typical dynamics of these types are: intellectual and introverted man falls in love with emotionally extroverted and intuitive woman. Or a person with many childlike attributes feels attracted to someone who is strong and parent-like and vice versa. These so-called parent–child relationships are not healthy, and they usually break apart once 'the child' grows up and wants a partner 'of their own age'.

THE STRUGGLE STAGE

'How on earth is it possible,' many people ask, 'that this magnificent stage of honeymoon can turn so easily into these horrible arguments and power struggles?' The answer to this questions is as simple as it is intriguing:

What attracts us most in our partner in the first place will annoy us more than anything later on.

How can that be? How can a rational man who was attracted to the emotionality of a woman suddenly dislike this very character trait in her?

In some respects, romantic relationships are a vicious thing because they provide us with a challenge we might not always be willing to meet. When we first fall in love, we feel drawn to someone who is different from us, and who has something we want to have because we miss it in ourselves. But as time goes by, these differences become a nuisance and we'd rather have someone who is more similar to ourselves.

The rational man mentioned above, for example, might be drawn sexually to an emotional woman, but in everyday life her emotionality may get strongly on his nerves. He might wish that she would solve disagreements and problems in the logical and unemotional way he is used to. And the emotional woman who felt initially drawn to his strength and composure will start to wish he could sometimes be a bit more empathetic and, yes – emotional. All this provides lots of good material for endless arguments where he can accuse her of lack of composure and logic, and she can accuse him of being stiff and lacking in empathy. Let me give you another example.

Jill is a hard-working and highly achieving woman who fell in love with Roy, who is just the opposite of her. He is fun-loving, and his career doesn't mean too much to him. Instead, he is into travelling and enjoying life. Jill and Roy had a fantastic honeymoon and spent two months together on a world trip that was like heaven on Earth for them, spiritually, emotionally and sexually. Jill could relax into her feminine side more than she had ever done before, and Roy enjoyed his masculine side as the confident tour leader who showed her the world.

Once they returned home, Jill rolled up her sleeves in her old hard-working way in order to organise the purchase of an old, ramshackle cottage that Roy was meant to renovate. As time went by, little was done in terms of work on the house, and while Jill went out to earn most of their money, Roy spent more and more time hanging out with his mates 'enjoying life'. You can just imagine the power struggles that followed.

This dynamic of getting annoyed with what you initially liked in your partner is totally unavoidable in every romantic relationship, and there is nothing we can do to get rid of it totally. After all, we wouldn't be attracted to someone who is totally the same as we are, and we feel strongly drawn only to people who are different from us and have in their personality what we are missing.

Yet it is these very differences that will present the biggest problems later on, which means that the more attraction there is between two people in the beginning, the more struggles they will face later on. If we understand this pattern, it will be much easier to deal with these problems when they hit us out of the blue and leave us puzzled and hurt.

It is not always easy to recognise that what annoys us now is actually what we fell in love with earlier. On the next page is a (non-exhaustive) list showing how the very character traits in your partner that appear highly attractive during the honeymoon stage may seem highly annoying later on.

Your partner's attractive character traits, with which you fell in love.	How the same traits get on your nerves later on.
Your partner is:	*Your partner appears later to be:*
Fun-loving and relaxed.	Lazy and disorganised.
Bubbly and vivacious.	Emotionally unstable.
Strong and reliable.	Stubborn and inflexible.
Calm and relaxed.	Boring and lacking in initiative.
Sexually passionate.	'Only' wanting sex.
Rich and successful.	Materialistic and superficial.
Wanting to be close.	Needy and dependent.
Caring and adaptable.	Weak and spineless.
Witty and humorous.	Avoiding any deep feeling.

The list could go on endlessly, but luckily there is one glorious exception. If your partner was very loving with you in the beginning, you will not experience any bad 'side-effects' of this beautiful character trait. Instead, you will continue to enjoy and relish their love, and you can use it to get over any of your other disagreements.

The key to getting out of any of the above dilemmas is to keep appreciating the character traits of our partner that we loved in the beginning, and work out compromises for those that have started to jar with our own personality. Often it will help enormously if we just point out that we can't expect each other to change or even to erase the very character trait we actually fell in love with.

If we can remember and value how much we initially loved what is now getting on our nerves, we have already laid a good foundation for finding a working compromise. If, for example, a bubbly and talkative woman feels she is still appreciated for her vivaciousness, she will probably be much more willing to give her spouse some silent minutes than she would be if she was constantly criticised for 'talking too much'. And her man will probably be ready to engage a little bit more in conversation with her if he still feels appreciated for his 'inner calm', rather than being attacked for being 'unresponsive and emotionally suppressed'.

The commitment to love each other and to grow in love in the struggle stage

You know that the honeymoon has ended when you suddenly look at your partner and no longer feel those lovely waves of delight for the mere fact that you've found this 'wonderful' person. In other words, at a certain point you will discover that your partner cannot provide you with complete and everlasting happiness.

For some people, this will come as a terrible shock, and some women will frantically start to try and 'change and improve' their man so that he can remain the source of all their happiness. Some men will secretly start to look for other women who could give them what their present partner isn't able to provide. However, now is the hour to prove that your commitment to love each other, and in particular your commitment *to grow* in love, is true and genuine.

Growing in love means embarking on the quest to find the source of everlasting happiness *in yourself*.

Two people who want to be soulmates are now challenged to give up unrealistic ideas about their partner, and to turn inside and try to find there what no other human being will ever be able to give them from outside. They are asked to follow a path of personal and spiritual development that will help them to find the deepest happiness within themselves, and to let go of wrong and overly idealistic expectations towards their partners that will only end in frustration. But even if two people turn inwards in order to find true happiness in themselves, the greatest challenge for them, as in every romantic relationship, is the commitment to love *each other*.

Truly loving each other means regarding the well-being of our partner to be as important as our own at all times and under all circumstances.

Did you know that it is actually impossible to win a fight in a love relationship? Whenever you successfully dominate your partner so that they do what *you* want, you will respect them less, so in effect *you* will be the actual loser of this fight. You will also lose their love, which makes matters even worse. Conflicts between partners can only be solved by finding compromises that make *both* people happy. This is easier than it sounds, and I will explain in more detail how to do it in the next chapter, which deals with constructive arguing.

For the time being, it is enough to say that two partners will only be able to get over the struggle stage successfully if their commitment to love is more than lip-service. There will be times when you could scream words of abuse at your partner because you are at the end of your tether. There will probably be times when you want to throw it all down and leave the house through the back door. And there will be times when you will feel tempted to close your heart forever, or even to do something really nasty to your partner in order to punish them for all the hurt they have inflicted on you.

If you are not able to contain these destructive impulses and remember that, despite all of your anger, in front of you is the person whom you actually love more than anyone else, you will destroy your relationship. This sounds brutal, but it is the truth. Our commitment to love starts first and foremost with our ability to refrain from being openly aggressive, cold-hearted and revengeful.

One of my Buddhist teachers used to say, 'One single really aggressive act in a relationship will destroy months of building trust,' and I definitely think that he is right. In terms of loving our partner, it is much more important for us to be able to swallow the spiteful remark that sits on our lips so nicely, than being able to give our partner the most loving compliments. As nice as such compliments are, they will be of little use if they are interspersed with destructive words and behaviour.

If we are successful at holding back our worst tendencies to be openly aggressive or indirectly cold-hearted, we can use our commitment to love each other to sit down with our partner and patiently work on *any* problems that arise. Sometimes it may be necessary to discuss our dissatisfying patterns for many days in a row; at other times it will be plain sailing for weeks and months on end. However, it is important to keep one thing in mind. Your problems will *not* go away if you don't talk about them. No amount of love and patience can erase the annoyance and frustration that inevitably arise when two people are trying to throw their lives together.

If you are the sort of person who can easily adapt to the needs of others, you need to be careful not to bottle things up and take your revenge indirectly by doing little annoying things, like leaving the house in a mess or constantly 'forget-ting' to do your part of the chores. Equally, you will not gain anything if you become aloof and withdrawn, and pretend that nothing gets under your skin. You will only pay for this later by either becoming very tired or making your partner even more angry.

You might even arrive at the point when you feel that no amount of good will and discussion helps you to get over the problems you face. At this point, your commitment to love each other will be strongly tested. You will find out whether it is strong enough for you to put all your pride on one side and seek the help of a professional relationship counsellor. Going to a therapist is not a sign that you and your partner have failed, or even that you can't be real soulmates. On the contrary, it is a sign that you are wise, and that your commitment to love each other is real and strong. In many cases, an unaffected and professional person can help two people to sort out in months what they couldn't sort out themselves in years.

Getting over the struggle stage is not easy. Particularly if you are both passionate and highly attracted to each other, you will probably have to sort out a lot of nitty-gritty, every-day issues. If, however, your commitment to love each other and to grow in love is strong, you will definitely master this stage and have many wonderful years to come, when you will be able to relish the harvest of the hard work that you are doing at the moment.

Unfortunately, the struggle stage is not one chunk of time that is over from one day to another; it has the annoying habit of coming and going in phases. You may think you are way into the lovely maturity stage, only to be hit by another episode of struggles. However, as time goes by most success-ful couples get better and better at arguing, and are able to sort out their disagreements more quickly and with less negative emotion.

The unavoidable merging process between partners in the struggle stage

The struggle stage usually happens after we have indulged in the honeymoon stage for some time, and many of our great initial needs to unite and merge are, at least in part, satisfied. With that another need emerges; this is the need to feel ourselves as our old identity again. We might then realise how *different* we are from our partner. This often comes as a shock, because during the whole of the blissful honeymoon stage we had entertained the illusion of being incredibly similar. When the realisation of our differences dawns, the struggles usually begin.

'But why do we have this struggle phase when the merging process is anyway unavoidable?' someone might ask. The answer is that the process of taking on our partner's character traits often takes place unconsciously, and that *consciously* we often resist becoming more like our loved ones. Although we might still find our partner very attractive, we also want to stay just as we are. Depending on the kind and strength of our ego, we will either fight tooth and nail to make our partner adapt *to us* rather than us adapting to them, or we will exert power more indirectly by being very stubborn and uncooperative. But the unavoidable merging process goes on whether we resist it or not.

Slowly but surely, we take on views and feelings about ourselves and the world, no matter how much we argue or whether we are aware of it or not. It is interesting to see that we often resist most ferociously in our partner what we have taken on unconsciously already. So in effect, we often fight ourselves as much as our partner. This dynamic often becomes apparent after a couple has split up. Suddenly the ex-husband starts taking more care of his health, the very thing he had constantly boycotted in his wife. Or the former girlfriend suddenly finds herself defending political views she had always resisted in her ex-partner.

Of course, people can try to rid themselves of what they have taken on from their ex-partners, and this is a wise thing to do if the traits are not really wholesome. However, often to their own surprise, men and women continue quite happily with what they have resisted so much when they were together with their partners.

Let me summarise: the unavoidable merging process that was the main attraction and delight in the honeymoon stage becomes the main challenge later on, when both partners wish to stay just as they are and have their partner adapt to *them* rather than the other way around. I have already explained the way out of this dilemma: it is to use your love and work out compromises that feel good for both partners.

The law of an even deal in the struggle stage

It is unbelievable how two people who want to give each other *everything* at the honeymoon stage can turn into those quarrelling brothers and sisters who argue about the tiniest perceived and imagined unfairnesses. 'You have eaten *my* piece of cake, and you have used *my* towel and you know very well that I don't like it!' 'Yes, but you always come home and throw *your* shoes in the hallway expecting *me* to tidy them up, and you *never* let me use the remote control and I don't like that either!' Does any of this sound familiar?

There is no other time when you have to be more meticulous about implementing the law of an even deal in your relationship than in the struggle stage. You can't expect your partner to remain as tolerant and generous as they were in the honeymoon stage, because the re-emergence of their ego is inevitable. On the other hand, if you are too self-sacrificing you won't win any spiritual points for the after-life either. Through self-denying behaviour, you will loose just as much as through being too egotistical, because your relationship as a whole can only thrive if a proper even deal is maintained. The following list gives you the most important guidelines to obeying the law of an even deal.

- **Both partners talk openly about whether they feel happy with the overall give and take in the relationship** What *feels* right for both partners is a good even deal.

- **Both partners make a conscious effort to ensure that their partner gets as much out of the relationship as they do themselves** For example, the partner who takes the initiative most, and who is most domineering by nature, should deliberately hold themselves back and ask their partner first whether they have some ideas of their own. Men have to be especially meticulous about this rule, as they have a tendency to assume that everything is all right as long as their partner doesn't complain.

- **Neither of the partners puts up with any perceived unfairness** For example, if one partner is very untidy the other partner should not just grumble silently. Instead they should challenge this behaviour and find a working compromise. The untidy partner can either learn to be tidier, or do something else in exchange, like the washing-up, for instance. Women have to be especially meticulous about this rule, as they have a tendency to interpret the even deal to their own disadvantage. It is, however, important for both partners to ask their spouse nicely and without criticism to fulfil their part of the even deal, to avoid even more arguments.

- **If one partner makes a major sacrifice for the relation-ship, the other should make an effort to give something back that equals this sacrifice** For example, if one person gives up their job and home in order to move in with their partner, the latter could give financial support or be much more tolerant and generous for a long while.

- **If children are involved and one partner stays at home** In this case, the even deal can become quite complicated. In my opinion, it only works if both partners agree that the child-rearing work is of the same value as the money-earning work. Therefore if the woman has looked after her babies and toddlers all day, she should have no more duties in the evening and at night than her husband. Obviously, there are no hard and fast rules, and each couple must work out for themselves what the even deal means for their situation. But the bottom line is that both partners should feel that the overall give and take is fair in their relationship.

- **Money** A particularly sensitive point for implementing the law of an even deal properly is money. The law in Great Britain says that in a marriage each partner owns the money they earn themselves, and that a house-wife or house-husband is only entitled to pocket money. In my view this is unacceptable, as it puts the stay-at-home partner in a dependent role, which will inevitably result in two outcomes: either resentment or withdrawal. Both these consequences are of course very detrimental to the ultimate aim of a soulmate relationship, which is love.

When a woman and a man earn very different amounts of money, or when one partner stays at home and looks after the children, the law of an even deal will only work if both partners throw all their money into one pot, and then distribute it in a way that feels fair for both of them. The couple can either make all bigger money decisions together, or if this would bring about too many arguments, deduct all the money for the house and family and simply split the rest in two.

The male–female polarity in the struggle stage

What has once been one of the greatest delights in the honeymoon stage can turn into one of the biggest problems in the struggle stage. I am talking about the fact of being man and woman. Being of the opposite sex to each other can provide a host of problems, although it was one of the biggest attractions at the beginning of the relationship. In particular, if a very masculine man and a very feminine woman arrive at the struggle stage, they will find that no matter how great their sex-life has been up to this point, they will have an awful lot of issues to sort out that stem from being so different.

As an example, at the beginning the erotic play between strength and surrender was a source of delight. Now she complains that he is rough and 'only wants sex', while he feels that she is withholding and wants things he doesn't know how to provide. During the honeymoon he could sit for hours and listen with fascination to her amazing feelings and intuitions, and she felt valued and appreciated. Now he wishes she would finally come to the point, so that he can give her some quick advice and go on and watch the football. All their differences in physique, thinking and feeling patterns that they found so wonderfully attractive in the honeymoon stage can now become a source of obstacles for the harmonious course of their relationship.

As explained before, the key to harmony will be to value your differences, which you fell in love with, and find working compromises for the parts that create friction. Let's look first at what that means for women:

One of the worst things a woman can do is to criticise or even ridicule her man's masculinity.

Criticising men is quite accepted in our society, and you only need to watch the commercials on the telly to find much ridiculing of everything that is traditionally masculine. However, if a woman does the same to her partner at home, she will have to pay a high price. By attacking his confidence, she will be destroying the very thing that could make her happy. No woman fancies a weak man who feels bad about himself!

It is particularly detrimental if a woman criticises anything that her partner *does*, even though this may be put across as seemingly harmless 'good advice' about how things could be done so much more quickly and better. The sensitive areas of a man are everything that has to do with his competence, such as his job, DIY around the house, and even the way he plays tennis or speaks a foreign language. Telling a man that what he does is not good enough, or even laughing about it, is just as bad as a man saying to his partner that she is getting fat and wrinkly. In other words, it's fatal.

I once knew a woman, Kathy, who had confided in me that her man Robert was 'no good in bed' because he had no confidence. However, whenever I saw those two in public, Kathy always made funny remarks at his 'masculine' expense. For example, if Robert wanted to do something that is traditionally masculine, like giving her a hand when she was entering a swaying rowing boat, she would ridicule his attempts at helpfulness and gallantry. She even declared openly that Robert was 'boring', while he swallowed all these attacks apparently unperturbed. I knew, however, that he had his silent 'revenge' at night.

As you can see, if Kathy had been wiser she would have nurtured Robert's masculine confidence by gracefully accepting his help and appreciating it, instead of destroying whatever little confidence there was in the first place. In this way, she might even have helped Robert to become a more successful lover.

Generally speaking, a woman should never stop appreciating and even relishing the very things and behaviour that make her man a man, and that she fell in (erotic) love with in the first place. If she does this skilfully and without neglecting to solve any problems in the partnership, her 'tactic' will result in having a supportive man by day and a confident lover by night.

Now let's look at the men.

One of the worst things a man can do is to criticise a woman for her emotions and her looks.

It is so easy for a man to look at a woman who is upset and tell her that she is overreacting. However, even if the woman agrees with his criticism, in the long term his lack of empathy and patience will always backfire, because she will take revenge either by withdrawing or by becoming very critical herself. A man should therefore always try to express how he values everything in his woman that makes her feminine, and he should never criticise her in this area.

Obviously, we can hurt our partner with *any* criticism in *any* area of their personality, but I think people strongly underestimate how vulnerable most men and women are in their gender identity. In order to continue to find joy and satisfaction in their relationship in general and in their sexual relationship in particular, people need nothing more than confidence in being attractive as a man or as a woman. Both genders therefore have to take great care not to destroy the very thing that would bring them so much joy if nurtured and appreciated.

The way out of all these dilemmas is as ever to sit down

together and painstakingly go through everything that creates dissatisfaction and hurt. If both partners can learn to communicate honestly but lovingly, any problem in a relationship can be overcome, be it in the sexual, emotional or communication area. It can even be fascinating to study each other's differences and to marvel at the complexity of what it means to be a woman or a man.

The end of the struggle stage
There are four different ways in which things may evolve from the struggle stage onwards. The partners are:

1. Unable to resolve their problems and split up.

2. Unable to resolve their problems and keep arguing. This is called a fight relationship, and in such a relationship the partners often have a sex-life that is sparked by the reconciliation after their frequent rows.

3. Unable to resolve their problems but stop arguing and live their different lives under one roof. Communication is reduced to a minimum and sexual relations stop. Such a situation is called a graveyard relationship.

4. Able to resolve all their problems and to continue to do so as soon as new conflicts arise. They will have a rich and inspiring communication, as well as a very satisfying sex-life. Only in a relationship like this will two partners have become true soulmates who have entered the stage of maturity. Congratulations!

THE MATURITY STAGE

Two people in a romantic relationship can only enter the maturity stage once the excited and blinding passion of the honeymoon, as well as the rough ocean of the struggle stage,

are safely behind them and they have entered the wide and
calm sea in the beautiful midday Sun. There might still be
the occasional thunderstorm, but on the whole it will be
plain sailing; the communication between the partners will
be more interesting and inspiring than ever, and their sex-
life will be deeply satisfying.

**The commitment to love each other and to grow in love in
the maturity stage**

The commitment to love each other and to grow in love is
the centrepiece of the maturity stage. At this point, the habit
of always regarding a partner's well-being to be as important
as one's own has become so ingrained that it has become
second nature. Soulmates wouldn't dream of subtly or even
openly dominating their partner, because it is so clear to
them that they can only be as happy as their partner is in the
long term. In this respect they almost feel like a being with
two bodies but only one heart, which will suffer even if only
a part of it is unhappy.

For the same reasons, soulmates wouldn't just give in
and submit to whatever their partner wanted, because they
are equally committed to loving themselves and unfolding
their own potential. Soulmates don't bottle up any negativity, but talk about everything that bothers them. When they
argue about a problem (or rather peacefully debate about
it), they are completely confident that they can always find
a good compromise that will make *both* of them happy,
because they have so often been through this process.
There is no longer any need for strong accusations or
complaints, because the focus is totally on the solution to
the problem, and this will usually be found in shorter and
shorter periods of time.

Soulmates are well aware that no other being can provide
them with everlasting happiness, and they don't expect it
from their partner. Instead, their focus turns to their path of
personal and spiritual development, which helps them to

find inner love and inspiration that they can feed back into their relationship as well as into other areas of their lives.

This process is very rewarding, and a person's ability to love will make them more and more able to see the beautiful divine nature of their partner. Nothing could be more bliss-ful than to move closer to your own inner divinity, and to see it more and more clearly in other people, too. A soulmate relationship in the maturity stage can be of great help in accomplishing this wonderful aim.

If two soulmates are lucky they will feel drawn to the same spiritual path, but that needn't be the case. If each partner's development is centred around becoming more loving, two people can be perfectly happy as soulmates even if they receive their inspirations from totally different sources. Soulmates know better than to resist new developments in their partner, and to judge anything that doesn't fit into their personal frame of mind as 'mad' or 'foolish'.

If one partner finds a way to develop inner peace and a more loving attitude to the world, the other partner will happily join in and follow their positive development. Real soulmates are even open to a partner's suggestions that they should try counselling, meditation or yoga in order to get over personal obstacles. Both partners thus inspire and help each other along their paths rather than holding each other back, as is so common with couples who get stuck in the struggle stage.

Finally, here is one of the best things about being soul-mates: over the years two people in a truly loving relationship will voluntarily take on more and more tasks and commitments in order to pass on the happiness they have generated through their own care for each other.

These commitments will go far beyond having children and looking after them. So much energy and happiness will be generated in a true soulmate relationship that both part-ners will have a great deal to give; they will not be able to stop themselves from passing on what they have found for themselves. Like cups that spill over, they will find projects and tasks of various kinds to be of help, inspiration and service to others and potentially to everyone in the world.

As an example, one soulmate couple I know (who have two children) have founded a spiritual centre and invite other people to it in order to learn spiritual laws and meditation. Another beautiful and radiant couple have helped and inspired each other to write and design a book together that carries a loving and thought-provoking message to the world.

Two people don't need to achieve spectacular success in order to be soulmates. However, the chances that they will grow beyond anything they thought possible are much higher if they have arrived at the maturity stage of a soulmate relationship.

The law of an even deal in the maturity stage
Soulmates are really good at implementing the law of an even deal in their relationship. You will not find a single soulmate relationship where one partner has a great and satisfying career, while the other is stuck in a situation that is oppressing and limiting in order to support their partner. Instead, both partners will be totally dedicated to the happiness of *each other*, and they will always make sure that each of them has a place and a task in the world they feel satisfied with. In order to achieve such an ideal situation, both people have to sit down again and again to discuss the different possibilities, and make every effort to work ceaselessly until they are *both* happy.

One of the big challenges of achieving a good and satisfying even deal comes when children arrive on the scene. Both partners suddenly find themselves having to cope with demands they'd never anticipated. 'Why did no one bother to tell us how excruciating this is?' they might frequently ask themselves, while they struggle to keep sane under the relentless bombardments of screaming demands.

No matter how much we love our children, having them will make any existing strain or problem in a relationship *worse*, be it financially, emotionally, sexually or health-wise. First and foremost, the lack of sleep will put us under a huge strain, and in most families there will be quite a few tears before the children have reached an age when they become easier. A marriage will only be enjoyable in these strenuous phases if both partners have learnt to communicate and work together effectively.

All this is not meant to deter anyone from having children, because on the plus-side children can also give us love and satisfaction beyond measure. However, the romantic idea that a baby can heal a stumbling relationship and bring two partners together could not be further from the truth. In reality the opposite is true. It is therefore wise for two partners to wait to have babies until they have safely reached the maturity stage, when they will be properly prepared for the unbelievable onslaught of joy, strain, love and effort that is awaiting them.

'But what if the wishes of the partners are too different to be reconciled?' someone might ask.

It is only when one or both partners starts to regard their own well-being to be more important than that of their partner that conflicts become unsolvable.

As long as someone regards their partner to be as important as themselves, there will always be a working compromise. Sometimes it needs time and effort to find this compromise, and sometimes people have to try out different things. As a last resort they can take it in turns to pursue their dreams – the partner who is not doing so can voluntarily stand back and support the one who is. If both partners whole-heartedly wish and pray for a genuine compromise, a satisfying solution will always be possible.

As time goes by, two people who want to develop will change and expand, and their life circumstances may change a lot as well. Compromises that worked previously will therefore need to be adjusted again and again. However, with a commitment to love and a clear understanding of the working of an even deal, even extreme situations can be mastered successfully.

Take for example the sad possibility that one partner has an accident, and becomes wheelchair bound and dependent on outside help. Is it possible to maintain the law of an even deal in such a situation? The answer is yes. If the injured partner is very appreciative of the help and care they receive from their partner, there is no reason why both partners shouldn't continue to have a deeply happy and loving relationship. If, however, the partner in the wheelchair becomes deeply depressed and resentful, and cannot appreciate the help of their partner, the situation will become much more difficult and might even lead to a break-up.

As you can see, it is ultimately the mental, loving attitude that determines whether two people have an even deal, and never their material and physical circumstances alone.

The unavoidable merging process between two partners in the maturity stage
As the years go by, partners in the maturity stage will take on more and more from each other and this will make them into more complete individuals. Slowly finding in yourself what you admired so much in your partner at the beginning is a wonderful process.

A rational and level-headed man, for example, may slowly get access to a much richer inner life through the loving contact with his more emotional wife. However, this process will not go so far as to make this man totally effeminate himself. His logical outlook on life will just be complemented and enriched in a healthy way because he will be more emotional, and this will make him more sympathetic and loving. In a similar way, his wife may slowly take on some of his more rational approaches to the unavoidable ups and downs of life, and she may discover that this positively complements her usual emotionality. She will gain in strength, but without loosing her femininity and liveliness.

The unavoidable merging process happens in the best and most harmonious way if two people love each other, and in particular if they have a loving sex-life that allows them to be very open and emotionally vulnerable. However:

The unavoidable merging process has one big drawback. As people become more similar, their attraction to each other wanes.

It is a well-known fact that the sexual and emotional magnetism of two people decreases over time, and there is absolutely nothing they can do about this whether they are soulmates or not. When two people take on the energy and character traits of their partner, they become more whole in themselves and there is less that they are missing in themselves. They are therefore both less needy, and accordingly the attraction between them decreases.

This sounds like bad news. However, soulmates have one big advantage that will compensate them more than enough for this drawback. As their magnetism to each other wanes, *their companionship will grow*. Being more alike can have many advantages, because it will make life so much more harmonious and easy. In a soulmate relationship, the attraction and passion of the honeymoon will be replaced with the deep emotional and sexual love of two people who are the closest friends possible.

On the other hand, two people in an ordinary relationship might argue forever about, for example, being 'too emotional or too repressed' while taking on these very character traits on an unconscious level – consciously, they will fight these traits in themselves as well as in their partner. On top of this unfortunate dynamic, as for other couples their attraction to each other will decrease. Unlike for soulmates, their love and companionship will *not* increase, and they will find themselves in either a fight relationship or a graveyard relationship. This is of course very sad, and there is only one way out of this negative development: a deeper commitment to truly love each other and the implementing of a satisfying even deal.

The male–female polarity in the maturity stage

As partners become more whole, women take on more masculine traits and men take on more feminine traits. No matter how macho a man might have been in his youth, if he lives for many years in a truly loving relationship with a woman, he will inevitably become more caring and gentle himself. Similarly, women who might have felt tender and shy in their youth will become genuinely stronger through the loving union with their soulmate.

This development of men and women becoming more whole and complete in a soulmate relationship is genuine and healthy. It is very different from having trouble developing confidence in your gender identity. A young man, for example, who comes across as very soft and caring may not even have access to his strong and dominant side because he is afraid it could be brutal and unacceptable. On the other hand, a man who has become more complete due to a loving relationship has access to both his emotionally responsive and caring side and his determined and dominant side.

Equally, a woman who comes across as very confident and bold might have great difficulties living her vulnerable and surrendering side. The wholeness of a woman who has lived in a loving relationship is different, as she can be determined and strong as well as surrendering and vulnerable. For each individual, these developments are very positive, because it makes them more independent as well as providing them with a much wider range of responses to the world.

As mentioned before, becoming more whole has the drawback of being less attracted to our partner for the simple reason that we don't need them so much any more. Sexual magnetism wears off particularly fast, and many couples are puzzled by how their initial infatuation with each other disappears so quickly and so completely. The merging process is completed most quickly on the sexual level, and takes much longer on the level of character. However, there is one area where the merging process never loses its fascination and is inspiring and delightful forever. This area is the heart and the love that springs from it.

If people are not aware of this dynamic, the decrease in their sexual infatuation can leave them very disappointed, and they might even look for new lovers. But if men and women change partners every time their sexual magnetism fades, they never come to experience how a change of focus from physical attraction to the attraction that stems from deeply loving each other can make sex more satisfying than ever. This wonderful development can be experienced even if two partners make love for many years.

There is a second dynamic that will help two people to continue to enjoy sexual passion and avoid the danger of becoming so similar that they are more like mates than lovers. To achieve this, it is important that both partners voluntarily stay in their gender, even if they could act in a more androgynous way. In other words, when a man shows more of his masculine side to his partner and she shows him more of her feminine surrendering side, they can experience sexual attraction even if they have been together for many years. Let me illustrate this with an example.

Sarah and Jim have a farm and they both have to work very hard to keep it going. Obviously Sarah can drive a car and the tractor as well, and she does a lot of hard work throughout her day. However, when Sarah and Jim go out, Sarah puts on her high heels and Jim opens the car door for her and drives her to a restaurant. On their romantic dates, Sarah never drives the car and never pays the bill. Instead, she allows Jim to care and provide for her, which he does with joy. For Sarah and Jim, all this is part of their sexual foreplay, and when they come home Sarah is in her feminine side and is able to joyfully surrender to Jim's sexual advances.

As you can see, when Jim and Sarah go out they are enhancing and strengthening their gender differences; this is the opposite of what they do in their everyday farm work, where they relate to each other more like mates. Far from being oppressive, their gender differences are very helpful for their loving sex-life.

Chapter 12

Turning Arguments Into Positive Development

I once listened to the talk of a renowned Buddhist teacher, who said that it is easier to reach enlightenment than to live in a truly loving and harmonious relationship. With all due respect, I don't agree with him. In actual fact, it is quite easy to have a wonderful romantic relationship once we have learnt to keep our commitment to love and carefully implement the law of the even deal in every respect.

Like everything in this world, however, relationships are not perfect. No matter how hard we try, there will always be occasions of conflict, emotional hurt and anger. If we don't have the skills to get over these hurdles, even the most perfect soulmate will be of little use. In order to acquire the ability to argue constructively and without hurting our partner, we need one thing more than anything: practice.

Most people thoroughly dislike conflicts and arguments, and do everything and anything to avoid them. In actual fact, many psychosomatic illnesses, addictions and neurotic symptoms are largely due to the fact that people try to suppress their negative feelings so as to avoid conflicts with other people. In order to turn arguments into positive mutual developments, we have to see them as positive opportunities to learn about ourselves, our partner and the way we communicate with each other, and we have to stop avoiding conflicts at any price.

THIRTEEN RULES ON ARGUMENTS

Rule 1 – Arguments are beneficial

I can't count the many people I know who follow a spiritual path of some kind and try to use it in order to make themselves immune to emotional hurt. I myself have tried to do this, and it goes something like this, 'I'll just pray and meditate and then the anger and the pain will go away and I won't need to deal with the person who hurt me directly.' Unfortunately, this equation rarely works out. In the worst cases, people become ill or neurotic, and in the 'best' cases they become aloof and unable to really enjoy intimate contact with others. We can only solve our problems with other people if we stop trying to suppress our emotional hurt and start to own our vulnerability.

Rule 2 – Feeling vulnerable is beneficial

The pain we feel in our heart when our partner hurts us is like a doorway that we need to go through in order to find a better way of communication. If we ignore and suppress this difficult feeling, the path towards a better situation will be lost. Let me put it a bit more drastically: the first time you find yourself trying to 'not care' any more when your partner has hurt you, you are hammering the first nail into the coffin of your relationship. It is not a good learning goal to become so tolerant and patient that you no longer mind when your partner is unloving, unfair or outright hostile. This attitude is bad for everyone involved: for yourself as it will be impossible to unfold your potential in such a negative atmosphere, and for your partner because you allow them to be selfish, which will cause them a lot of suffering in the long run.

Rule 3 – Never bottle up conflicts

The bottling up of conflicts can never be beneficial, because it leads to resentment and the silent growth of distance and boredom between two partners. Although it can seem like a strain to have to sit down again and again and go through the same old annoying pattern that keeps happening between you, in the long run it will definitely pay off.

One word of warning: before anyone sees these first three rules as advice to take out their frustrations on their partner as and when they arise, have a look at the next rule.

Rule 4 – Being openly aggressive is extremely detrimental

There are two things that are more destructive for a relationship than anything else; they are cheating and being openly aggressive. If we want to live in a soulmate relationship, it is absolutely crucial that we have ourselves under control in terms of sexual and aggressive urges.

For people who have trouble controlling their temper, there is a host of therapies that can help them to get over this problem, ranging from relaxation techniques through counselling to flower remedies. However, none of these practices will work as long as they are ignored. People can learn to control their negative emotions, but they have to actively want to do so, and use the help that is offered to them. Only then will they be able to ask their partner *calmly* to talk about anything and everything that is bothering them in order to find a good compromise.

Rule 5 – Don't pay anything negative back, but insist on amends

Controlling your anger doesn't mean that you have to silently swallow anything negative that comes from your partner. It is totally appropriate to tell your spouse that you are angry if this is the case. However, you should not give in to the urge to say something mean or to punish your partner in any way for the bad things they have done to you. The reason for this it that taking revenge will lead into a downwards spiral of increasing negativity.

Instead, you need to apply the law of an even deal by insisting on apologies and amends. Only when you have received appropriate 'compensation' for your emotional hurt can you be truly good again with your partner. You can also be very proud of yourself because you have resisted your inner negativity, and opened up the way to a more positive development with your partner. Let me illustrate this with an example.

In a couple I know Arthur, the husband, sometimes looses his temper and says things he afterwards regrets. His wife Betty deals with this situation neither by shouting back nor by silently suffering. Instead, she tells him how annoying she finds his uncontrolled anger and insists on getting not only a sincere apology, but also a present of some kind in order to feel good again. She has also agreed with Arthur to take classes in relaxation, which they enjoy doing together. As you can see, for them the even deal is restored, and they are actually benefiting from the situation by learning to relax together.

Rule 6 – Regard the well-being of your partner to be as important as your own

If you think that Arthur's behaviour is unrealistic and cannot be expected from the average man, remember the main prerequisite of a soulmate relationship. Only if we regard the well-being of our partner to be as important as our own do we truly love them; in that sense, Betty and Arthur's behaviour is totally appropriate.

It is absolutely crucial that we admit our mistakes as soon as we realise we have made them, and do whatever we can to make good and apologise. A soulmate relationship is not a place for 'proud' men and women who can't admit when they are wrong. In addition, if Betty 'just' forgave Arthur's outbursts of uncontrolled anger without getting an apology and a present, she would probably take her revenge subconsciously by becoming cold or sabotaging. 'Just' forgiving will only work when we have a lot of distance from the person who has hurt us and are able to let them go. But if we want to live with someone under one roof, and to keep making love to them, both partners must be able to *always* admit their mistakes and make amends. Once this is done to both partners' satisfaction, the whole episode should be forgiven and forgotten and mustn't be regurgitated during any future arguments.

Rule 7 – Keeping your agreements is the key to peace

All of what was said above will be of little use if both partners cannot keep their agreements. Take for example one of those ridiculous but typical conflicts about how certain things should be done around the house or with the children, and imagine that after arguing a bit both partners find a good compromise. Then imagine that one or both partners constantly breaks this agreement. Not surprisingly, there will be constant frustration in the relationship.

Arguments are only beneficial if both partners can use them to agree better ways of doing things in the relationship. But if one or both partners cannot learn their lesson and keeps breaking the agreements, it will be hard to find lasting peace. In order to become totally reliable, two people need nothing else than a clear determination. For some people this is very easy, but for others it is hard work, although they can learn it just like anyone else.

Rule 8 – You cannot change your partner (although you can try)

You definitely cannot change anyone against their will, but that doesn't mean that you should never try to influence them. On the contrary, two people who want to grow in love together need to inspire each other to make changes that can feel uncomfortable at first.

Inspiring your partner to change themselves is a high art, and you need to be very skilful to do it. The best way is to 'praise and admire' your partner into changing themselves. For example, if you want your male partner to be more communicative, tell him as often as possible how much you love your conversations with him and how much you value the way he talks to you. Or if you wish that your female partner could be less inhibited in bed, tell her as often as possible what a fantastic lover she is. Talking in this way is not manipulation but a good relationship skill, because the chances are that you will get a more talkative husband and a more passionate wife, which is good for everyone.

If, however, you feel really frustrated with the behaviour of your partner this tactic won't work, and it would also interfere with rule three, concerning not bottling up conflicts. In this case, go to rule nine to find out how to communicate successfully about your problems, so that everyone will end up being happy.

Rule 9 – Don't criticise, but speak about your wishes

This rule is extremely important, because apart from betrayal and aggression nothing causes more emotional hurt in a relationship than criticism. If you tell your man that he did a lousy job around the house, or you tell your woman that her upset emotions are annoying, the chances are that you will have a mega-conflict with a lot of either anger or ice-cold silence.

It is much more beneficial to talk about yourself and your wishes. For example, you could calmly say to your man, 'Would you mind having another look at this issue because it is still not working?' or to your woman, 'Please, darling, can you calm down so that we can talk about this in peace?' If you are really angry you could say, 'I am upset because this is still not working. I wish for it to be done properly,' or 'I find it difficult to talk to you when you are so upset. I wish to talk in a more peaceful atmosphere.'

If you talk about your wishes instead of criticising your partner, it will be easier to sit down together and discuss things in a better way. In the words of one of my teachers: 'We must never tire of writing a user-friendly manual about ourselves for our partner, even if they are slow to learn.'

Rule 10 – Don't interpret, but ask

Whenever two people communicate, everything they say goes through an internal process of interpretation. For example, when a man *hears* his woman saying, 'I am so tired and exhausted,' he might *interpret* this as 'She is criticising me for not helping her enough,' and *react* in a resentful way. This is of course the last thing his partner desires. Equally, if a woman *hears* her man saying, 'I'd like to read the newspaper now,' she might *interpret* this as 'He finds what I have to say boring,' and *react* in a very upset way. This is of course what would annoy her partner more than anything.

In both cases, it would have been much more beneficial if each partner had *asked*, 'Do you want to say I am not helping you enough?' or 'Does that mean that you find me boring?' The partner could then have quickly dismissed their worries.

Some people think that they never misinterpret anything and always understand exactly what their partner is trying to say. Nothing could be further from the truth. We *must* interpret everything we hear and we do this by using everything we know about the other person, the tone of their voice and their body language. Communication is not otherwise possible.

If we can remember that there is no communication without interpretation, we will become much more alert to the possibility that we could interpret things in a more negative way than they were actually intended. Then we would also understand that it is much wiser to *ask* whether our partner actually means the negative things we seem to understand, instead of assuming that we know exactly what they want to say. In this way, numerous misunderstandings and a great deal of bickering can be successfully avoided.

Rule 11 – Don't threaten, but inform

Sometimes you may come to a point in your discussion when you and your partner are stubbornly stuck in your positions and not ready to give even one inch. This is the time when some people start to threaten: 'If you treat me this way you can sleep in the lounge,' or even, 'If you continue like this I will get a divorce!' However, if you threaten your partner in this way, you will either strengthen their rebellious side and make them even more stubborn, or force them into submission and receive their revenge later through emotional coldness and unsupportive behaviour.

It is much better to speak about yourself and your feelings, and *inform* your partner instead of threatening them. For example, you can say, 'When you behave like this I find it so hurtful that I can't imagine being close to you again, let alone making love. I'm not saying this to threaten you; it is just the way I feel and it hurts me myself.' Or, 'If you don't do this for me I will lose all my motivation to do something else for you. I am not saying this to blackmail you, but it is how I honestly feel and I find it very sad.' If you inform your partner in this way, they won't need to become even more stubborn and rebellious. Instead, you may open up a way for them to understand you more deeply and to look for a better way of tackling problems.

Rule 12 – Make it up before bedtime

This is a very important rule because it puts a time limit to all anger and hostility. It is best to agree it when you are at peace with your partner, so that in times of war it will help you to find at least a cease-fire before you go to bed.

It is, in fact, extremely beneficial to agree as many rules as possible to limit negativity, like never using abusive language with each other, never shouting and never punishing each other with silence. Even if one or both partners breaks these agreements, they can apologise and make up. An argument is only completely resolved when everyone who needs an apology or compensation has got what they need to feel good again, and when both partners have agreed a better way of behaving and communicating to avoid future disharmony. When both partners are able to stick to this agreement, this helps to reduce the overall negativity in a relationship.

Rule 13 – Keep the romance alive

As every health practitioner knows, prevention is better than treatment. In terms of avoiding arguments in a relationship, this means making an effort to keep the romance alive. Sweet little gestures and presents, and loving hugs and kisses that are not intended as sexual foreplay, go a long way to keep power struggles at bay. Similarly, compliments about looks, character and achievements help to keep both partners feeling happy and appreciated. However, the biggest romantic gift is of little use if two people cannot give each other sympathy.

Women in particular feel more loved and romanced through the loving and empathetic understanding of their man. In most couples, however, it is the woman who craves romance more strongly and the man who forgets it more easily. This is not due to ill-will; it's merely how men are. Unfortunately, this puts a woman into an awkward position, because if she initiates romance too much it will not feel romantic at all. The archetypal romantic gesture comes from the male to the female, and not the other way around.

The way out of this dilemma is for the man to accept that the woman needs more romantic gestures and sympathy than he ever thought possible, and for the woman to accept that the man needs the occasional reminder. She can then ask him directly for sympathy, or casually imply that she would like a romantic present. The man should take these hints very seriously and respond to them as well as he can. It can help if he puts a reminder in his wallet or on his to-do list.

All this can seem a bit contrived at the beginning, but couples who work in this way are certainly much happier than those who insist that everything should go totally 'naturally'. This usually results in the woman being resentful about the fact that her man is so unsympathetic and un-romantic, and the man feeling unappreciated and confused.

Sympathy and the occasional romantic gesture (even if they are asked for by the woman) can boost the love and sex-life of two soulmates in many ways, and they can prevent a lot of bickering or boredom that occurs when two people loose their 'romantic touch'.

THREE ESSENTIAL TECHNIQUES FOR SUCCESSFUL ARGUING

You probably think that these thirteen rules are all very well in theory, but that that they are of little use once you and your partner find yourself in a heated argument. You are right – applying the thirteen rules needs dedication and practice, and for most people developing the ability to use them takes time.

For those heated moments, I am giving you just three techniques; you can learn to remember them even if you are furiously angry.

1. Symbol therapy

Symbol therapy has proven incredibly helpful for a huge range of problems, and it can be used to lessen the negativity in an argument and come to a solution relatively quickly. My husband and I work with healing symbols when we feel a conflict coming on, and they have never failed to improve the way we communicate. How does it work?

You or your partner need to sit down and go through the following little practice in order to ask your Higher Consciousness for a healing symbol to overcome the suffering of destructive arguing. Then both of you need to work with this symbol in the recommended way for two minutes a day, or each time you feel an argument coming on. You will then find that you are much more able to peacefully resolve your issues, instead of getting terribly angry with each other.

Symbol Therapy for Successful Arguing

Part 1
Decide which partner will ask for your healing symbol. The other partner can slowly read out the following exercise.

- Relax in way that is convenient to you.

- You are now ready to come into contact with your Higher Consciousness. See your Higher Consciousness as an angelic being surrounded by light, or as a beautiful shimmering light that has a living and loving quality. Feel how you are embraced by the love and support of your Higher Consciousness.

- Ask your Higher Consciousness: 'Can you please give [name of partner] and me a healing symbol to overcome our suffering from arguing in a destructive way, for the best of all beings.'

- You might be shown one or several symbols (for example flowers, gems or geometrical forms), and you should pick one that you find attractive and that has a beautiful and bright colour. Acknowledge the very first thought or idea of a symbol that comes into your mind. If you are not sure whether you have received the right symbol, you can check with your Higher Consciousness. Watch out for an inner feeling of 'yes' or 'no'.

- When you have received a healing symbol describe it to me.

- If I am not happy with it can you please ask for another one.

- Once we are both satisfied, we thank your Higher Consciousness for its help.

Part 2
For both partners.

- Visualise your healing symbol in the middle of your own chest, in your heart, and when you breathe out exhale the colour of your symbol throughout your body, into the area surrounding your body and towards your partner. When you breathe in, just enjoy the presence of your symbol in your heart. Then exhale the colour and the positive qualities of your symbol again. Do this in a **loving** way for two minutes.

- Visualise or feel your healing symbol in your heart and breathe out its colour and good qualities for two minutes a day, or whenever you feel an argument coming on. Visualise your symbol in exactly the form it was given to you by your Higher Consciousness, and never change it yourself. If it seems to change of its own accord, don't allow this to happen but always go back to its original form.

---

2. 'You, me solution'

Many arguments go on and on for the mere reason that both partners cannot agree on an agenda. For example, the man wants to find a quick solution while the woman wants to share her feelings. In this way, they can drive each other to distraction. It goes something like this:

Woman: 'I am upset that you left the kitchen so untidy.' (I want to talk about *my* feelings.)

Man: 'But you left the garage in such a mess yesterday and I had to tidy it all up afterwards.' (I want to talk about *my* situation.)

Woman: 'Now you are changing the subject. Let's talk about the kitchen.' (I still want to talk about *me*.)

Man: 'Okay, I'll go and do it then.' (I want to talk about *the solution*.)

Woman: 'Look, it really hurts me if you don't tidy up the kitchen. I don't feel appreciated.' (I still want to talk about *my* feelings. I want to feel understood.)

Man: 'You are always making a drama out of everything. I could complain about many things if I wanted to.' (I want to have a quick *solution*.)

Woman: *Starts to cry.* (I still want to talk about *me* and my feelings.)

Man: 'Look, I already said I will do it. You are driving me mad.' (I still want to talk about *me* and the *solution*.)

Woman: *Crying even louder, shouts,* 'You are driving *me* mad! Why can we never talk about anything in peace?' (I still want to talk about *my* feelings.)

Man: *Leaves the room slamming the door.*

The reason why this couple cannot talk peacefully is that they are trying to discuss different topics. She wants to talk about herself and her feelings and is less interested in a quick solution, and he wants to talk about his situation and about the solution. They will never come to an agreement by arguing in this way.

Now let's look at how this argument would have developed with the 'you, me solution technique'. It goes like this.

Woman: 'I feel upset that you left the kitchen so untidy.' (I want to talk about *my* feelings.)

Man: 'But you left the garage in such a mess yesterday and

I had to tidy it all up afterwards.' (I want to talk about *my* situation.)

Woman: 'Now you are changing the subject. Let's do the "you, me solution technique", okay? Can I talk first?' (I want to talk about *my* feelings and can we agree on this?)

Man: 'Okay.' (I agree; let's talk about *your* feelings.)

Woman: 'Look, it really hurts me if you don't tidy up the kitchen. I don't feel appreciated.' (I want to talk about *my* feelings. I want to feel understood.)

Man: 'I am sorry that I forgot and I do appreciate how you look after the house.' (I want to talk about *you* and your feelings.)

Woman: 'Okay.' ... *Break* ... 'Now, what about you?' (Let's talk about *you*.)

Man: 'I am okay. I'll go and tidy up the kitchen, okay?' (I only want to talk very little about me. Can I go on to the *solution*?)

Woman: 'Okay. Is it good again between us now?' (Let's talk about the *solution*.)

Man: 'Yes.' *Gives her a kiss*. (Let's talk about the *solution*.)

These two arguments don't look that different, but they are actually a world apart.

If you find you have similarly annoying patterns with your partner, you merely need to agree beforehand that you will argue in an orderly manner – first about one person, then about the other and then about the solution. It is so simple that even children in a sand-pit can use this technique. And it will bring peace to many situations that would otherwise have got out of hand.

3. Time out

Here comes the lifesaver for when you get so angry that nothing else helps. Leave the room! Go around the block and work with your healing symbol until you have calmed down, and then return and try again. It is as simple as that, and it can save your relationship!

Like the other two techniques, this one should be mutually agreed *before* you find yourself in the middle of a row, and once one partner announces that they need a break to get themselves under control, the other partner should be supportive.

Chapter 13

From 'Having Sex' to 'Making Love'

For many people, sex is great fun during the first few months of a new relationship. This is a time of an abundance of sexual hormones, which make sure that both partners experience an exhilarating attraction that they can use to explore all kinds of sexual possibilities.

Sooner or later, however, problems such as premature ejaculation or an inability to reach an orgasm can greatly inhibit the lust for making love, and even later, almost every couple experiences a more or less disappointing decrease in sexual attraction to each other. This can be the result of the unavoidable merging process that every couple has to go through, or it may be due to unresolved conflicts and creeping emotional withdrawal from each other. When we experience such problems, the challenge starts.

As is the case with all conflicts you may have with your partner, it is important not to see this obstacle as a mere nuisance, but to also look at it as an interesting possibility to grow and to unfold more of your dormant potential. In this way, your sexual relationship with your soulmate can be a path of learning. This will be greatly rewarding if you don't dodge a few problems that you may encounter.

There are basically three areas in any romantic relation-ship that need to be addressed in order to have a truly satisfying sexual experience. The first challenge is to resolve all your emotional problems with your partner and to not allow a build-up of resentment that would make intimacy impossible. The second challenge is to make things work sexually between you and your partner on the physical level. This means both partners being able to have an enjoyable foreplay, a long enough intercourse and a pleasurable orgasm. But that is by no means all.

The third challenge is to experience a deep emotional and even spiritual dimension in your sexual encounter that goes far beyond just having orgasms, no matter how many. This emotional satisfaction can only be found by bringing your sexual energy into your heart. When you and your partner can learn to use sexual feelings to increase and enrich your love for each other, this will more than compensate you for the unavoidable decrease of physical attraction that comes with the years. In this way, 'having sex' will truly turn into 'making love'.

The previous chapter about arguing has dealt with the first challenge of resolving emotional conflicts. The follow-ing two sections deal with the other challenges.

Making It Work Sexually

Like all the other areas of a relationship, the sexual area works best if two people really love each other and apply the law of an even deal carefully. This means that when it comes to sex, the satisfaction of our partner should be as important to us as our own.

This seems to be pretty obvious advice – in an ideal world, no one would want to have sex in a very selfish or overly self-denying manner. However, the reality is that too many women don't have the confidence to ask to be fully satisfied in every sexual encounter, and too many men don't make the effort to make sure that this happens. The result is disappointment and a smouldering grudge in women, and annoyance, guilt and confusion in men.

Talking about sex

The first step out of the above dilemma is to talk to your partner about your emotional and sexual needs and desires. Having a sexual relationship can be an exciting journey of ever-new possibilities, and the phase of sexual exploration doesn't need to be limited to the first few months of a new relationship. If you keep trying out new things, your sexual relationship will also be much less at risk of becoming stale and boring.

When talking about sex, it is extremely important to avoid criticising your partner's sexual performance in any way. Almost everyone's self-confidence is built on thin ice when it comes to our behaviour in bed. It would therefore be very unwise to weaken your partner's sexual self-esteem and thus make them more uptight and inhibited in bed. If you want to suggest something new, you should never point out what you *don't* like about your partner's sexual behaviour; only talk about the things you *would* like.

It will often be the woman who wants to have things differently, and she needs to be very careful to talk in an appreciative and loving way to her partner. The man should be as accommodating and loving towards her wishes as he can be, and should not take them as a sign that he isn't a good enough lover. Instead, he could try to see her suggestions as a way of making their sex-life better as a whole. If one partner has a sexual wish the other finds hard to comply with, both partners should always try to find some sort of compromise. Often it will be enough to experience the good will of our partner in order to feel satisfied.

People who find it difficult to talk about sexual matters can get hold of one of the numerous books about better sex and read them either together or apart. Without having to say anything, you can point to certain paragraphs or pictures and tell your partner whether you like them or not. Reading books about sex is also a good way to find out what you would like in the sexual area overall, because no one can be expected to know all these things just by themselves.

Timing is another important aspect when it comes to talking about sex. Almost the worst time to talk about your sexual wishes is just before or just after making love – but talking about them during making love is worst of all. The best time to communicate about these things is usually some-time during the day.

In the next step you can try to put the things you have talked about into practice. In most cases this will be a process of trial and error, and it is incredibly important to maintain humour and a loving attitude in all your endeavours to enrich your sex-life. Nothing will hinder your sexual satis-faction more than being impatient and demanding, and nothing will help it more than being laid-back and playful.

Men are like fire and women are like water

The old Chinese practitioners of Taoism knew a lot about sexuality and how to use it for longevity and spiritual advancement. One of their basic ideas is that women's sexual energies are like water and men's are like fire. The fire needs just one spark in order to be ignited and burn fiercely, and in the same way many men just need one sexual thought or one gaze at a naked woman in order to feel aroused and be ready to make love. Women, on the other hand, often need longer to come to full sexual arousal, just as water needs longer to come to a boil. Therefore most women need the loving and skilful sexual seduction of a 'hot' man in order to become really aroused themselves.

It is important to understand this difference between men and women's ways of becoming ready to make love so as not to get stuck in the age-old argument that 'he thinks she

needs too long and she is irritated that his foreplay is too
sexual and impatient'.

**As a rule of thumb: in order to have satisfying foreplay,
women need romance and men need patience.**

If you are a man, try to never tire of telling your partner
how much you love her and how beautiful she is while gently
stroking or massaging her in a non-sexual way. She will soon
let you know that she is ready for more. If you are a woman,
try to relax into the sexual advances of your partner like you
would surrender into a delicious hot bath after a cold day
outside.

Once a woman is aroused and the water of her sexual
energies is 'boiling', she can be much more enduring than a
man, whose sexual energy can come to an abrupt end like
fire that has burnt up a handful of straw. The old Chinese
experts in sexuality taught that the sexual pleasure of a fully
aroused woman can be up to seven times stronger than that
of a man.

It is the man's task to learn to be more enduring in order
to enhance his partner's sexual joys and then participate in
them. By being very loving, a man can virtually feed on the
sexual pleasure and rapture of his partner, and in this way
both partners can have a wonderful experience. A woman,
on the other hand, can only come to the height of sexual
arousal through fully surrendering to the sexual activity of
the man. If she can fully give herself without any holding
back, her sexual joys will multiply. This will be wonderful for
herself as well as being the most beautiful gift she can give
her lover.

If the love-making goes on for long enough, the male-
domineering and female-surrendering roles can suddenly
swap and the woman at the height of her arousal can become
wild and domineering herself. This can be very enriching to
partners who are confident in their gender identity. This
swap in gender roles is very different from that engaged in

by women and men who don't dare to fully live their femininity or masculinity and take on the opposite gender identity as a defence.

A woman whose sexual energies are 'boiling' can experience many orgasms, and virtually every part of her body can be orgasmic. She can come again and again, but instead of being less aroused she will be even more horny shortly after each orgasm. A man, on the other hand, usually experiences a total loss of his sexual desires as soon as he has ejaculated, just as fire will be cold as soon as it is extinguished. It is therefore important for a man to learn to control his orgasm in order to prolong the love-making until he and his partner are both fully satisfied. The best way to do this is to have breaks during intercourse, as described in the next section.

Once a man has had an orgasm and his fire is extinguished, he has the much joked-of desire to roll over and sleep because his energy is totally depleted. But the woman usually isn't sleepy at all after a good love-making session. Her 'water' cools down only slowly, and she wants to cuddle and talk. If the man understands the difference between his 'extinguished fire' and her 'still warm water', it will be much easier for him to resist his desire to sleep and stay awake for another ten minutes – the two can then hold each other and talk about their experiences.

As you can see, the metaphor of fire and water beautifully explains the differences in the sexual energies and behaviours of men and women in all four phases of love-making: foreplay, intercourse, orgasm and the time after making love. This image also suggests the differences between men and women that can be used to enhance the sexual pleasure of both. On the other hand, if we expect our partner to be 'just like ourselves', we will experience many disappointments and much heartache as well.

The female orgasm

The female body is a miracle when it comes to sexual arousal and orgasms. It is virtually made for sex. Differently from a man's body it has numerous erogenous zones, and it can be aroused and brought to orgasm in many different ways. Men who have made love with many female partners know that there are no two women who climax in exactly the same way. There are as many forms of female orgasm as there are women, and every woman can learn to climax in many different ways if this is what she desires.

Unfortunately, men like Sigmund Freud have tried to tell women what a 'real' orgasm has to be like, and even more unfortunately, too many women have tried to listen to them. Instead of tuning into their own inner wisdom, they have tried to adapt to the sexual norms imposed by male authorities, and have thus lost a great deal of their own ability to experience sexual pleasure.

The first step to experiencing wonderful orgasms is to look at your own peak sexual experiences with confidence and see them as your own way of having an orgasm that is fully valid and good. There is no 'orgasm exam' for women to pass, and whether your peak experience is mild, rapturous, clitoral, vaginal or from any other part of your body, *you* and only you have the authority to declare it a full and real orgasm.

There are basically two main forms of orgasm, genital orgasm and whole-body orgasm, and neither is better or worse than the other. The genital orgasm can be reached through manipulating the sex organs, and the whole-body orgasm can only be reached through a deep emotional and bodily surrender. The wonderful female body even has special organs for both forms of climax – the clitoris for the genital orgasm and the erogenous zones all over the rest of the body for the whole-body orgasm.

Both men and women can experience these two forms of

climax, and they can also learn to have multiple orgasms. However, this is much harder for a man because he has to learn to come without ejaculating, which is not easy, to say the least. Women have a great advantage in this respect, because they can fully let go into their sexual experience without any risk of denying their partner sexual pleasure by coming too early. Women also have a greater talent for surrendering, which makes it even more likely that they can experience the genital as well as the whole-body orgasm.

Reaching a clitoral orgasm is relatively easy. All you have to do is to have a hot bath, screw off the showerhead of your shower and direct a strong beam of warm water against your clitoris. Then indulge in some nice sexual fantasies and enjoy! When your orgasm comes easily in this way, you can try to imitate the sensation of the water with your fingers, or teach your partner to do the same. However, there is absolutely nothing wrong with stroking yourself while your partner enhances your joy by pleasuring your nipples or vagina with his fingers, tongue or penis. Whatever works is good!

The whole-body orgasm is more a matter of emotional attitude than of a 'right' technique. You can actually experience such a climax without any techniques at all, and even without having sex or masturbating. Women have experienced whole body orgasms during meditation, while breast-feeding their babies and even during childbirth. And obviously they can have many such orgasms during making love.

What is needed to experience the whole-body orgasm is surrender. This is an attitude of letting go and allowing yourself to be taken over by a force that is stronger than you. The more you can put your ego to one side and allow yourself to be overcome by the sexual pleasure your partner is giving you, the more likely it is that you will experience a multitude of whole-body orgasms. It definitely helps to groan and moan loudly, and to let your body move spontaneously in sexual and ecstatic movements.

The attitude of surrender comes from loving your partner with all your heart, and completely giving him your body and your sexual ecstasy as your most precious gifts.

Then your pleasure will mount and finally explode in a way the captures your whole body as well as your heart. Whole-body orgasms can be gentle and mild, or overwhelmingly strong – you could even find yourself starting to cry as a result of your deep surrender.

Obviously, there is no situation more likely to produce wonderful whole-body orgasms than a deeply loving soul-mate relationship.

MAKING LOVE BETWEEN SOULMATES

Exploring all your sexual possibilities and finding more and more ways to have stronger and even multiple orgasms can be greatly exciting and satisfying, and can keep two people sexually attracted for a long time. At some point, however, almost every couple experiences a decrease of sexual chemistry, and no amount of sexy lingerie and sexual techniques can hide the fact that the excitement is not what it used to be.

Both partners will also find that there will be a growing number of reasons for *not* making love, like physical ailments and the wear and tear of daily life, and there will seem to be ever-fewer occasions when life is good enough to easily relax into erotic pleasure. On top of this, both partners will often experience a lack of meaning in making love mainly for the sake of physical pleasure. After having had hundreds or thousands of orgasms, it can seem less interesting to have just one more. Therefore many people in soulmate relation-ships will feel a need to explore the deeper meaning in having sex with each other.

The desire to find a deeper purpose for their love life can be a very rewarding development if two people don't dodge this challenge. Soulmates, with their dedication to grow in love, will understand quite easily that the solution to this problem is to join heart and genitals, love and sex in a more intense way. As I have explained, the main reason for the decrease in lust for each other is the unavoidable merging process. Once two people have taken on enough sexual energy from each other, their need for more will simply decrease.

This process is complete for most couples after approximately a year. However, the energy exchange between the hearts of two people will never be complete, and it will stay exciting and wondrous no matter how many years they spend together and how many times they make love. Therefore, if we can bring our feelings of love more deeply into our sexual encounters, having sex will never loose its attraction. Sleeping together in a more loving way will also serve the highest purpose of two soulmates, which is to love and to grow in love.

Bringing sex and heart together in a deeper way is something one can easily talk about, but it is more difficult to put into practice. Soulmates, like everyone else, are subject to the wear and tear of daily life; they have their conflicts, and they may have to work hard to earn their money. It therefore cannot be said often enough that the whole-hearted dedication of both partners is needed if they want to develop in a way that will ensure that love permeates their whole life.

Bringing love and sex together in a more intense way

If we want to bring more heart into our sex-life, we must first of all understand that the foreplay starts in the morning, after waking up. If there is little or no affection during the day, it is less than likely that there will be lots of love during sex, and indeed, if there will be any sex at all. Women in particular need to feel emotionally secure and loved in order to be able to fully open up to their lover. A tender hug and an 'I love you' for no special reason during the day will go a long way in making a woman ready for sex many hours later. For the same reasons, two people need to have mastered the challenge of resolving all their issues in a harmonious way during the day, so that they are ready to completely open their hearts during making love at night.

Two soulmates must also resist the natural tendency to become more and more like mates as their merging process becomes more complete. Instead, they need to make a conscious decision to go on to delight in their gender differences and the erotic sparkle that comes from being opposites. (Let me stress again that this applies only to those gender differences that bring joy, rather than suppression.)

If these three conditions have been met, two soulmates can go on to actually bring sexual energy into their hearts during love-making. The following exercise is derived from Taoist sexual practice; by working with it you can use sex in order to increase your ability to love and thus enhance and accelerate your whole spiritual development.

To Use Sex To Grow in Love

- Initiate and start making love in the way that feels emotionally and sexually fulfilling for both of you.

- After some time of active love-making, one of you suggests a break. Rest together in a comfortable position and let your sexual energy spread throughout your whole body. Feel how every part of your body becomes deliciously sexualised. Then bring your attention to your heart in the middle of your chest and the love you feel for your partner. Express this love in your gaze, in loving sounds and words, and in the way you hold and gently stroke your partner.

- Before the man looses his erection, resume your active love-making and take the love you felt during your break into your whole experience. Go on expressing your loving feelings as well as your sexual feelings in a way that feels good for both of you.

- After some time, rest again and as before spread your sexual energies throughout your whole body. Then concentrate on your heart and the love you feel for each other. Express your feelings in the way described above.

- Continue to alternate during breaks and active love-making.

- Finish your love-making in the way that feels good for both of you.

If you don't have a partner at the moment you can do this exercise on your own while masturbating and thinking of your desired soulmate. Alternate as described between masturbating and spreading your sexual energy throughout your body and concentrating on the love for your imagined partner in your heart.

Masturbating in this way (but without climaxing) can also be a good practice in cases where one partner has much less sexual desire than the other. If the less sexual partner masturbates without having an orgasm during the day, they are often much more ready to make love in the evening.

It can sometimes be a bit difficult to interrupt your passionate love-making in order to feel the love in your heart. It's not a tragedy if you get carried away by strong sexual feelings, but you will lose an opportunity to strengthen what is more important than anything in the big scheme of things: to love and to grow in love.

If you can bring more love into your sexual encounters, you will find that having an orgasm will become less and less important. The whole experience can become so delightful and even blissful in itself that having an orgasm or not might not make any difference any more. If you feel this way, it can be beneficial to not climax. This advice can seem a bit puzzling, particularly if you have spent a long time improving and deepening your ability to have orgasms. Not climaxing can be wise for two reasons.

Firstly, the sexual energy you have drawn into your heart will not be diffused in the discharge of energy that typically happens when we have an orgasm. Instead, the delightful feeling you have generated with your love-making will vitalise your whole being, and quite possibly inspire and enrich your life for days to come.

Forgoing your orgasm will also help you to maintain the sexual attraction to your partner. You will feel more eroticism in your relationship, which you can use to grow even more in love.

One last word of warning: like any other act of renunciation, letting go of your orgasm will only be beneficial if the desire for this is genuine and is not the result of self-suppression. What really matters is our ability to love ourselves and others, no matter whether we have an orgasm or not.

If you and your partner like to make love in the way described, your sexual encounter can become like a meditation that is powered by your strongest energy, which is your sexual drive. In this way you can greatly accelerate your spiritual development, and both you and your partner can become the most joyful, compassionate and loving people, who can bring an abundance of positive energy into the world.

I wish you the best of luck!

Index

About the Author

Ulli Springett is the author of *Symbol Therapy* and *Make Your Dreams Come True*, both published by Piatkus Books, and *How To Find Your Soulmate*.

Ulli offers life-coaching, counselling, e-mail coaching, talks, workshops and meditation groups and can be contacted via e-mail at: ullispringett@yahoo.com. Please visit her website at www.authorpages.co.uk/ullispringett